REFLECTIONS

OF THE

WEAVER'S WORLD

REFLECTIONS

OF THE

WEAVER'S WORLD

THE GLORIA F. ROSS COLLECTION

OF

CONTEMPORARY NAVAJO WEAVING

Ann Lane Hedlund

DENVER ART MUSEUM

This exhibition and its accompanying catalog have been made possible by the National Endowment for the Arts and the Denver Metropolitan Scientific and Cultural Facilities District.

Editors: Marlene Chambers and Steve Grinstead
Designer: Mary H. Junda
Photographer: Lloyd Rule

Portraits and other context photographs: Ann Lane Hedlund
Photograph, p.48: Howard Jones, Howard's Photography; courtesy Russell Foutz Indian Room, Farmington, New Mexico
Loom illustration and map: Anna-Maria Crum

Cover: Teec Nos Pos/Red Mesa rug (detail), 1988, Mamie P. Begay (9)
Cover close-up: Elsie T. Tom's hands

Bertha Little rug study lent for the exhibition by National Park Service, Hubbell Trading Post Historic Site

Printed in the United States of America
Library of Congress Catalog card number: 92-72353

Published by
Denver Art Museum
100 West 14th Avenue Parkway
Denver, Colorado 80204
Distributed by
University of Washington Press
ISBN 295-97231-9

PARTICIPATING MUSEUMS

Denver Art Museum
Denver, Colorado
July 11–October 4, 1992

The Heard Museum
Phoenix, Arizona
Spring 1994

Renwick Gallery of the National Museum of American Art, Smithsonian Institution
Washington, DC
Summer 1994

Joslyn Art Museum
Omaha, Nebraska
Fall 1994

National Museum of the American Indian, Customs House Facility
New York, New York
Winter 1994/1995

ABOUT THE AUTHOR

Ann Lane Hedlund is research associate at the Denver Art Museum and associate professor of anthropology at Arizona State University, Tempe, where she also directs the museum studies program. She received her Ph.D. in anthropology from the University of Colorado at Boulder and is author of *Beyond the Loom: Keys to Understanding Early Navajo Weaving* (Johnson Books).

FOREWORD

With this exhibition and catalog, we celebrate an extraordinary, decade-long collaboration between collector Gloria F. Ross, anthropologist Ann Hedlund, the Denver Art Museum, and the Navajo artists themselves. The Gloria F. Ross Collection of Contemporary Navajo Weaving grew out of Mrs. Ross's professional interests as a successful tapestry *editeur*. She first consulted Ann Hedlund, a specialist in Navajo textiles, because she wanted to commission Navajo weavers to produce tapestries based on Kenneth Noland designs. By then, Gloria Ross had already been working with leading American artists for more than twenty years, translating their designs for weavers to recreate as tapestries in her own New York workshop and in well-known weaving centers abroad. Over the next two years, as Professor Hedlund introduced Mrs. Ross to Navajo weavers and their multifaceted world, a close personal friendship grew up between the two women, and they eventually began to discuss the possibility of forming a collection of contemporary Navajo weaving at an art museum.

The Denver Art Museum has had the great good fortune to be selected as the site for this collection—primarily because of its long history of valuing, collecting, and exhibiting the art of native peoples in the larger context of world art. Gloria Ross founded the collection here in 1980 with the gift of several rugs she had acquired on trips to the Navajo Reservation and established a generous fund to build a permanent collection of contemporary Navajo weaving. Ann Hedlund was to contribute her expertise by selecting and documenting future additions to the collection on her frequent field travels.

The collection that has evolved stands as a remarkable testament to the creative vitality of the Navajo weaving tradition today. Now, in a catalog that explores the social, economic, and cultural context in which this weaving tradition thrives, Professor Hedlund gives us a rich new insight into the artists and the beautiful textiles they have created. We are most grateful to Gloria Ross for gifts that expand the scope of our Navajo textile collection into the present. In recognizing the living continuum of the aesthetic impulse, through all times and cultures, she makes a significant contribution to the future we all share.

Lewis I. Sharp, Director
Denver Art Museum

ACKNOWLEDGMENTS

Many people helped me gather information and impetus to write this book and curate the traveling exhibition. I would like to thank one and all for generously sharing their ideas, energy, and support. As Navajos say in gratitude, *Ahéhee'*! In the final analysis, of course, any errors here are my own and belong to no one else.

At the heart of this endeavor, many, many weavers and their families invited me into their homes, shared their lives and aspirations, and gave this project their personal attention. I especially want to thank the weavers represented in the Gloria F. Ross Collection of Contemporary Navajo Weaving—Bessie Barber, Alice Begay, Amy Begay, Gloria Begay, Mamie Begay, Mary Lee Begay, Helen Bia, Mary Brown, Irene Clark, Sadie Curtis, Susie Dale, Isabell John, Bessie Lee, Teresa Martine, Kalley and Jennie Musial, Grace Henderson Nez, Irene Julia Nez, Barbara Ornelas, Rose Owens, Ella Rose Perry, Marjorie Spencer, Daisy Tauglechee, Jennie Thomas, Lillie Walker, Audrey Wilson, Elsie Wilson, Larry Yazzie, Philomena Yazzie, and Ason Yellowhair. Rose and Robert Owens have taken me and my husband into their large extended family and have encouraged and assisted me in innumerable ways; their daughter Gladys Owens Mazerbo and their grandson Marvin Owens also deserve special thanks. My life is enriched immensely by all of these very special friends. *Ahéhee'*!

Gloria F. Ross has been a vital partner in my fieldwork since 1979. As instigator and collaborator on the Gloria F. Ross Collection of Contemporary Navajo Weaving, she is responsible for my being able to assemble the textiles presented here. Her high professional standards were measuring sticks for every aspect of the project from field collecting to museum conservation, exhibition, and publication. Her thoughtful questions and observations as we traveled together over miles of reservation roads and corresponded between Arizona and New York provided important stimulus and crosschecks to my research. Her joy in good craftsmanship and design taught me to look at things more closely and see them more acutely. Her friendship and *joie de vivre* have enlivened every moment that I've spent on this project. *Ahéhee'*!

Since my undergraduate days, Joe Ben Wheat has shared his groundbreaking research and clear thinking about both historic and contemporary Southwestern weaving with me and has encouraged my own work in innumerable ways. The late Kate Peck Kent, too, provided provocative thoughts on weaving. John Adair, Jan Bell, Noel Bennett, Kate Duncan, Linda Eaton, Margaret Hardin, Russ Hartman, Nancy Parezo, Terry Reynolds, Peter Welsh, and many other colleagues stimulated my research through helpful comments and observations. Elizabeth Welsh read the entire manuscript in its early stages, asked insightful questions, and gave me valuable editorial guidance. Conservator Jeanne Brako was technical consultant for the exhibition mounts. *Ahéhee'*!

Many traders, gallery owners, and other dealers in Navajo textiles generously shared their knowledge and understanding of Navajo weavers and current market trends. I'm especially grateful to John Barr, Sande and Bill Bobb, Bruce Burnham, Jackson Clark, Jackson Clark II, Ed and Jed Foutz, Kathy Foutz, Mr. and Mrs. Russell Foutz, Dan Garland, Steve Getzwiller, Russ Griswold, Tom E. Kirk, Bill Malone, Mark and Janet Shipley, J. B. Tanner, the late Bill Young, John Young, Tom Wheeler, and Les Wilson. Many others in the business of buying and selling rugs spent time talking with me, too, and I gratefully acknowledge their help. *Ahéhee'*!

Kenneth Noland generously donated his interest in *Nááts'íílid*, woven by Irene Clark, as well as two relevant *maquettes*, to the Gloria F. Ross Collection. Mr. and Mrs. Jeffrey M. Kahn kindly contributed Jennifer Musial's rug. Jeffry A. and Carole A. Katz provided me with useful comparative material from their collection. *Ahéhee'*!

Over the past decade, it has been a distinct pleasure to work with the Denver Art Museum, and I'm grateful to the entire staff for many professional services and personal kindnesses. Special thanks go to director Lewis Sharp for his enthusiastic support and to Nancy Blomberg, associate curator of native arts, for her dedicated and skillful management of all aspects of this project. Richard Conn, then curator of native arts, played a significant role in establishing the collection in Denver. *Ahéhee'*!

Gretchen Johnson and Jan Jacobs were invaluable in developing educational programs for the exhibition. Marlene Chambers and Steve Grinstead ably took my manuscript from ideas on paper to polished book. Photographer Lloyd Rule is responsible for the formal portraits of the collection reproduced here, and Mary Junda designed their splendid setting. Cynthia Nakamura, Photography Department manager, cheerfully performed yeoman duty in the studio as well as the office. Exhibition designer Jeremy Hillhouse and his staff prepared a gallery environment worthy of the weavings that are the *raison d'être* for the project. *Ahéhee'*!

The Registration and Collection Management offices facilitated the innumerable arrangements that proliferate in the preparation of every traveling exhibition—my thanks to L. Anthony Wright, Debra Ashe, Pamela Taylor, Mitchell Broadbent, Matthew Crespin, and Melissa Dougherty. Conservator Carl Patterson supervised the mounting of the collection for display, and Kelley Cooper, Marie Fraley, Lorraine Friedrich, Helen Furlong, Nancy Iona, and Phoebe McFarlane generously volunteered their time to mount each textile for the exhibition. *Ahéhee'*!

It was a special treat to work with Nicholas DeSciose, independent filmmaker, and Dan Labbato, Paul Kane, Rick Rubin, and Soren Bredsdorff in preparing the documentary video that accompanies the exhibition. *Ahéhee'*!

The National Endowment for the Arts furnished partial funding to the Denver Art Museum for the traveling exhibition and this publication. Other funding came from the Denver Metropolitan Scientific and Cultural Facilities District, which underwrites many significant programs for Denver-area audiences. The Department of Anthropology at Arizona State University, where I am an associate professor, provided time to further my research, and the College of Liberal Arts and Sciences supported my summer fieldwork with two minigrants and a grant-in-aid. *Ahéhee'*!

Jan Downey, Julie Katz, Nancy Mahaney, Ellen Moore, Rebecca Rich, and Michael Williams—graduate students in the museum studies program at Arizona State University—ably assisted in transcribing tape-recorded interviews, tabulating field data, testing educational modules for the exhibition, and conducting essential curatorial and clerical tasks. Becky Rich was especially helpful in facilitating the textiles' photography. Lori Weidner, a Navajo playwright, translated my 1988 field tapes from Navajo to English. *Ahéhee'*!

My parents, Jim and Doris Hedlund, sister Carey, and parents-in-law John and Marjorie Schweitzer have consistently encouraged and supported my professional life. And most especially, Kit Schweitzer, my husband and frequent companion on reservation trips, endured my long-standing preoccupation with this project with more good humor than I might have, had the tables been turned. In addition to myriad observations about contemporary Navajo weaving and weavers, he has given me invaluable insight into the creative process and into myself. *Ayoo ahéhee'*!

GENESIS of a COLLECTION

The Gloria F. Ross Collection of Contemporary Navajo Weaving at the Denver Art Museum now holds thirty-eight rugs and tapestries woven by thirty-two women and one man during the 1980s and early nineties. The collection's beginnings are intertwined with another project with separate but related goals—the creation of a series of original tapestries commissioned by New Yorker Gloria F. Ross, designed by contemporary painter Kenneth Noland, and woven by several Navajo women. Despite their distinct natures—one a museum collection of Southwest ethnic design and the other an art venture originating in New York—both collections are collaborations that have continued for more than a decade. Both projects also depend upon the appreciation of Navajo weaving within a unique cultural context and within a broader aesthetic framework. Our story begins with the Ross/Noland/Navajo project and leads to the development of the Gloria F. Ross Collection of Contemporary Navajo Weaving at the Denver Art Museum.

In the summer of 1979, when I was working for the Navajo Tribal Museum in the heart of the Navajo Reservation, I received a message from New York City. A *bilagáana*[1] woman named Gloria F. Ross wanted to commission Navajo weavers to make a series of tapestries designed by American painter Kenneth Noland. A widely experienced tapestry *editeur*, she would translate Noland's designs into appropriate colors, textures, and dimensions for the weavers. Using

Gloria F. Ross in the yarn room at Burnham Trading Post, Sanders

images by Romare Bearden, Jean Dubuffet, Robert Motherwell, Louise Nevelson, Frank Stella, Jack Youngerman, and others, Ross had been collaborating with artists for over twenty years, first in her New York workshop and then through commissions to weavers in Edinburgh, Scotland, and Aubusson, France.[2] Now, she wanted to work with Native American weavers and selected Kenneth Noland as designer. Known for his bold, shaped canvases with concentric circles, cat's-eyes, chevrons, diamonds, stripes, and plaids, Noland balances finely tuned color combinations against strong geometry. In these paintings and in other work such as handmade paper, color and shape dominate. With Morris Louis, he had been a pioneer and well-known proponent of the Washington Color Field School that emphasized, as he once said, "color and surface, that's all" (Waldman 1977:33). Ross selected Noland's work for a collaboration with Navajo weavers because the upright Navajo loom and its particular type of tapestry weave tend to produce

flat, even surfaces enlivened by blocks of pure, unshaded color. She saw rich potential for translating Noland paintings into this Navajo medium. Did I know anyone with whom she might work?

I explained that Navajo weavers do not work in studios or *ateliers* like those Ross knew in Europe. Surrounded by children and grandchildren, goats and sheep, Navajo weavers typically work in their homes. They proceed at their own pace, fitting weaving into a wide array of other household and community activities. In most cases, the weavers themselves choose all of their materials and work "on speculation," as it were; they usually wait until a rug is cut off the loom before seeking a buyer.

Navajo weaving, like life on the reservation, I told Ross, places high value on individuality and autonomy. Weavers work from their own heads and their wealth of experience, not from paper *maquettes* or cartoons (as they are called by European tapestry weavers). They are accustomed to letting a design grow on the loom and to following a pattern in their mind, as the interlaced yarns shape it. They might not make a rug exactly as she specified. Their designs and color combinations derive from complex origins—indigenous basketry motifs coupled with borrowed Pueblo Indian, Spanish, Anglo, and Middle Eastern patterns—but these borrowings are modified and reshaped into a fully Navajo expression.

I also explained that many women still use their native Navajo language and do not speak English fluently; communication could be a challenge. On the other hand, there are Navajo weavers with college degrees and international travel experiences. In their case, finding time in already busy schedules could be the challenge.

Bessie Watchman working at home, Kinlichee

Spiritual concerns also might limit collaboration. In addition to avoiding excessive behavior of any kind, traditional weavers do not work at certain times, such as during preparations for a ceremony, in the final stages of pregnancy (lest the rug be unfinished when the baby is born), and during frequent summer rainstorms. Although few, if any, woven designs are held sacred, some women harbor strong feelings against weaving certain types of designs—those that completely enclose a figure, for instance, and those designed by someone else. I was, of course, simplifying matters, because my fieldwork on the Navajo Reservation had shown me, if nothing else, that weavers actually take a wide range of approaches to their craft.

Working with Navajo weavers, as in any cross-cultural enterprise, would be an adventure in flexibility and self-discovery. Listening to and learning from their views would have to take precedence over expressing our own interests and wishes. Would New Yorker Gloria Ross and Navajo weavers find common ground on which to make commissioned

tapestries? And would I, a museum anthropologist, be willing to collaborate on a project that could directly influence the craft of a Native American society?

On reflection, I agreed to become part of the project. The eclecticism and diversity of current Navajo weaving might well serve as an asset to the Ross/Noland/Navajo project. The weavers' strong identities and self-determination that I'd originally listed as potential obstacles became the very reasons to collaborate. Ultimately, my decision to participate in this venture was based on four premises.

First, the Navajo world is resilient and eclectic. While Navajo weavers have opened themselves to a wide variety of influences over the 300 years since they adopted the craft, they have maintained a characteristically Navajo sense about their work. I judged that this integrity would survive yet one more introduced set of images and that the weavers would adapt the new elements to their own purposes. Their intense interest in the process of weaving prompts them to make textiles with diverse images. Furthermore, because the Navajos' approach to most woven designs is secular and nonsymbolic, it seemed likely that Noland's designs would be accepted alongside familiar patterns.

Second, Navajo weaving is a practical, commercial enterprise; many weavers want the income and professional recognition such a project would bring. Most Navajo families mix different income sources—full-time wage labor, part-time and seasonal jobs, stockraising, farming and household gardens, arts and crafts, welfare and other federal and tribal subsidies may all contribute to an extended family's collective support. Familes range from very poor to quite well-to-do, depending largely on how much land and livestock they control and by

their access to wage-paying jobs. Weaving, as part of the Navajos' mixed economy, can make the difference between a tenuous and an adequate living for many families.

Third, autonomy and individualism are a prominent feature of Navajo culture. Shouldn't the weavers themselves have the option to accept or reject Ross's proposal?

And fourth, collaborating on the Ross project would offer me new opportunities for studying the relationships between Navajo weavers and their patrons and clients. The Ross/Noland/Navajo project would extend my research and provide another way to compensate some of the weavers with whom I'd been working.

Gloria Ross and I made our first joint expedition to the Navajo Reservation during the summer of 1979. In advance, she sent out several small paintings by Kenneth Noland to serve as models for the Navajo weavers whom we would select. I will never forget picking up a modestly wrapped package at the Greyhound bus station in Gallup, New Mexico, and unpacking Noland's two gemlike artworks— one was handmade, tinted paper, the other a painting in acrylic. Ross and I traveled extensively across the reservation that summer. We visited many of the weavers who had collaborated with me on earlier research projects, and we saw many rugs in progress. Several weavers agreed to create large tapestries from Kenneth Noland designs. Ross worked with them on overall dimensions and motif proportions, yarn weights, color selection, and a multitude of essential details. Several "Navajo/Nolands," as we came to call them informally, were produced for Gloria F. Ross Tapestries by the end of the year. Equally important, Ross recognized the weavers' own artistic talents and bought several rugs woven with the weavers' own designs.

During our long drives through Navajo country, we compared notes about weaving history, American Indian cultures, the art market, museum activities, travel in other parts of the world, our families and friends, and anything else that came to mind. A special friendship was swiftly and smoothly formed. My anthropological world in the Southwest and her art-oriented world of the East Coast made perfect counterpoint. Ross appreciated the visual aspects of weaving and of our surroundings, while I was more attuned to their cultural and historical significance. She related to the personal elements of each weaver's life, and I often focused on their collective experiences. She taught me to test my own judgments about aesthetic quality over and over again; I showed her how to see the weavers' work through the eyes of an anthropologist, how to look at the independent and internal merits of another culture's aesthetics.

On our second reservation trip in March 1980, Ross put several more Navajo/Nolands into production and acquired more contemporary Navajo rugs. By then, she had studied Navajo weaving and added that knowledge to her extensive understanding of tapestry and fine arts. And, even though she wasn't necessarily interested in acquiring a large personal collection, the collecting bug had struck.

As time went on, Ross and I began to talk about the possibility of establishing a collection of contemporary Navajo weaving at a major art museum. We agreed that the ultimate purpose of such a collection should be to exemplify the best weaving we saw in progress on the reservation. But how should "the best" be defined? Ross's primary intent was to assemble Navajo examples that could be presented as fine art in urban art museums, where their visual qualities would be judged by the same criteria as Euroamerican

fine and decorative arts. Her experienced eye and aesthetic sensibilities would establish a baseline for selection from this perspective.

My ethnographic knowledge of the weavers and their backgrounds, their technical capabilities, and weaving trends would add a cultural dimension to the selection process. We would seek one-of-a-kind experiments, as well as rugs representing known styles. We would highlight the individual creativity of the weavers. Always, we agreed, the collection should demonstrate the technical proficiency and eclectic spirit that characterize recent Navajo weaving.

The size and diversity of the Denver Art Museum made it our choice for this collection of significant contemporary Navajo textiles. Most important, the museum has a tradition of honoring native peoples and their art as an integral part of its larger mission. Founded in 1893, the Denver Art Museum held the first, and for many years the only, collection of native art acquired by an art museum according to aesthetic, cultural, and historical criteria. The Department of Indian Arts, as the Native Arts Department was first called, was established in 1925 expressly to preserve and showcase Native American contributions to the world of art. Frederic H. Douglas, curator of the department from 1929 to 1955, was responsible for the development of a major collection of "outstanding examples of almost every style and medium in which Native American artists worked" (Conn 1979:16). The Ross collection would build on the museum's own superb collection of Southwestern weaving.

By the end of 1980, Gloria Ross had selected several Navajo rugs from her recent reservation purchases as gifts to the Denver Art Museum and had established a generous fund there to create and curate a permanent

collection of contemporary Navajo weaving. I was to purchase additions to the collection during my travels to various parts of the Navajo Reservation. Goals for the Gloria F. Ross Collection of Contemporary Navajo Weaving were drawn up with Richard Conn, then curator of Native Arts and now chief curator, and three successive directors of the museum. The explicit guidelines have not changed since their inception:

- To acquire some of the finest specimens of modern Navajo weaving available today in order to represent the best artistic and aesthetic qualities of the craft;
- To illustrate current trends in Navajo weaving by seeking as wide a range of styles, materials, and techniques as possible, including both representative ("typical") and aberrant examples;
- To acquire pieces with as much documentation as possible about their construction (*i.e.*, native names, type of wool and yarn, dyes, etc.), their makers (ethnographic background, individual biographical data), and their culture (historical, economic, symbolic significances);
- And lastly, to complement the present permanent collections with examples that extend stylistically and temporally the interpretations of Navajo weaving already possible.

The Gloria F. Ross Collection of Contemporary Navajo Weaving is thus the result of a unique collaboration between donor, researcher, weavers, and museum. It is also the product of a dialectic between Ross's art historical (aesthetic) approach and my anthropological (cultural) perspective.[3] In this collection, Navajo weaving can be seen as a visually exciting art, emerging from and still enmeshed in a rich cultural matrix. Like artists of any other time and place, the weavers are individual creators who contribute to the contemporary art world even as they respond to and draw from it.

Putting together the Ross collection at the Denver Art Museum has raised difficult questions about selecting and interpreting native objects and describing the lives of those who make them. For instance, there is considerable challenge in attempting to collect "the best" or "the finest." A search for the "modern masters" of Navajo weaving today is bound to be quixotic, for there are many well-qualified contenders and many cross-cutting criteria to employ—technical proficiency, designs, colors, materials, historical connections, family background, previous accomplishments. And the search may begin from many viewpoints— art historian, anthropologist, private collector, businessperson, museum curator, relative, neighbor, community member, fellow weaver, and others. Native Americans, Anglo-Americans, Europeans, and groups with other ethnic origins hold different views, and so do members within each of those groups. Clearly, there is no single set of objective criteria for collecting.[4]

The Ross collection represents a meld of professional and personal decisions. The broad goals that were outlined at the project's outset always guided choices. One of the most important standards—visual impact—was a personal one, developed by examining literally thousands of rugs over the past two decades and gauged very directly by personal preference. Technical proficiency (appropriate thread counts, straight edges, evenness, unusual materials, and so forth) was necessary but not alone sufficient. Cultural and biographical criteria (trends represented, regional styles, family lineages, prizes received, for example) added weight. We also took into account how each rug contributed to the collection as a whole—how it fit with other pieces and what kind of interpretation it could add to the overall story of weaving's vitality.

Listening carefully and trying to represent the diverse viewpoints of Navajo craftspeople have posed the most exciting opportunities in this project.[5] As Canadian museum director Michael Ames (1986:46) avows in *Museums, Anthropology and the Public,*

> There are many voices, many stories. They do not add up to one consistent view, nor should they, because they represent different people with different interests and experiences. We nevertheless need to listen. The articulation of native points of view may serve to remind us that outsiders do not have the final word. It is the continuing interaction between these various perspectives that is important.

Unlike many Navajo blanket and rug collections described from traders' and collectors' perspectives, documentation for the Ross collection views weavers as active protagonists rather than passive recipients of and respondents to outside influences. Because I'm not a Navajo weaver, I do not write from the weavers' perspective, but I have tried to observe and listen closely and have begun, at least, to understand how little of the weavers' own perspectives are represented in other collections or publications. The Ross collection reflects my interpretations of the many voices that belong to contemporary Navajo weavers. Indeed, these weavers and their families are part of the intended audience for this book and exhibition, and so our dialogue continues. I look forward eagerly to the time when Navajo weavers organize museum collections, exhibits, and catalogs and independently take museum projects in new and unforeseen directions.[6] New directions might mean entirely different intentions, goals, or formats, and I relish thoughts of what I cannot yet imagine.

The weavers represented here were involved directly in practical aspects of the Ross collection. Whenever possible, weavers were told their work was going to the Denver Art Museum for an eventual book and exhibit and asked in what other ways they would like to be involved. Each gave the museum express written permission to reproduce the work; for issues of privacy, some declined to have their pictures taken or included here. Those who agreed received prints of my photographs of themselves, their families, and homes. They also reviewed and made suggestions about what was written about them. Because of local rivalries, family jealousies, and financial concerns, two weavers—a mother and daughter—declined to have details of their careers included here. Although they originally agreed to the use of their names, they later asked for anonymity.[7] With a characteristic respect for autonomy and without a hint of resignation, other weavers counseled us to do the project our own way. "It is up to you," they often said.

We assembled the Gloria F. Ross Collection in the daunting knowledge that those weavers selected could easily become singular icons for Navajo weaving. Hundreds of others equally deserve recognition. The weavers chosen are unquestionably among the very best; the point to emphasize is that there are still others, meritorious but unnamed here. The Ross collection is not meant as a template for collecting "name" weavers or their specific styles of rugs.

Certain tactical questions also arose in the collecting process—not just who and what to represent, but how to buy? Whenever practical, we bought directly from the weavers. In an effort to document marketing as part of the weavers' world, rug purchases were also made from an array of outlets—small trading posts, large rug stores, elite off-reservation galleries, the Crownpoint Rug Auction, the Museum of Northern Arizona's Navajo Show, and Santa Fe's Indian Market. A persistent challenge required balancing three goals: to maximize funds set aside for purchases, to pay prices that honor weavers and encourage them to do their best work, and to minimize interference in the local economic system in which local traders are long-term participants. Weavers and traders alike agree that establishing an appropriate price is a difficult undertaking.

There is, also, the inevitable matter of influencing the weavers' future work through our selections. Ames (1986:48) aptly notes that "anthropologists through their curatorial and research activities are actively contributing to the development of the phenomena which they are so busily collecting and studying." Placing special orders and selecting rugs that meet certain technical and aesthetic criteria can have significant, but unpredictable, impact on future production as buyers' standards and expectations become reinforced in the weavers' minds. In fact, such suggestions, inadvertent or intended, are often welcomed by weavers eager for feedback from the market. Reassuringly, Navajo weavers' responses remain, as always, delightfully their own—it is "up to them" to decide what ideas to use and what to discard.

I first visited the Navajo Indian Reservation in 1970 when, as a geology student, I spent two weeks hiking in the canyons around Navajo Mountain. In the next few years, I learned to spin and weave, Anglo-style, while briefly living on a sheep farm in Canada; I switched from studying rocks to anthropology; and I made many visits to Navajo country. The information about Navajo weaving and culture I present in this catalog comes principally from the weavers with whom I have worked since the mid 1970s. Seeking as many perspectives as possible, I talked not only with weavers and their families, but also with nonweaving Navajos, traders, collectors, reservation school

teachers, and tribal officals; I studied trading post ledgers and weavers' scrapbooks; I attended sheep shearings, community meetings, and rug auctions. My earliest fieldwork involved the study of blankets and rugs in museums and a survey of traders and their rug inventories on the Navajo Reservation. For my doctoral dissertation, I gathered biographical and cultural information from weavers in one community, and I learned about their learning and teaching networks, divisions of labor and roles of relatives, religious and spiritual issues, marketing patterns, and economic concerns (Hedlund 1983). I also documented the range of loom types, other tools, raw materials, and techniques in use during the 1970s and eighties (Hedlund 1987), and I regularly surveyed the state of the art across the reservation (Hedlund 1988). For several summers I worked for the Navajo Tribal Museum in Window Rock, where I examined and documented the collection of Southwestern blankets and rugs and involved local weavers in the museum.

"Participant observation" is the major method of anthropological fieldwork, and that is how most of my time on the reservation is spent—watching, listening, and taking part in activities—in order to learn about Navajo families, their weaving practices and preferences, and the larger context in which they live. Being a *bilagáana* handspinner and weaver myself, I often work alongside Navajo weavers, with less need to talk than to contribute through activity. As one weaver aptly observes, "It is not a Navajo way to ask questions." Being present for everyday and special events in many homes, helping cook meals, herd sheep, and corral cattle, giving people rides to the store, school, or hospital, setting up my own loom, and being tutored by my adopted Navajo "mother"—as well as the more formal activities of keeping

fieldnotes, gathering census data, and making maps—all have contributed to my learning about weavers and their work, to choosing pieces for the Ross collection, and to writing this book.

The weavers' own words, used throughout this book, were recorded on tape or in my handwritten field notes and represent more weavers than those with rugs in the Ross collection. Many conversations took place in Navajo with on-the-spot translations or verbatim translations made later from tape-recordings. Because English is spoken as a second language by many Navajos, I have corrected grammar slightly in direct English quotations to clarify meaning and to represent the speakers accurately as articulate individuals when speaking their native language. Brackets indicate my editorial additions. Although all quoted speakers gave me permission to repeat their statements, I have preserved their anonymity when requested. For Navajo terms, I have used Young and Morgan's orthography (1980), with the exception of the "slash *L*" and the symbol for nasalized vowels.

The next chapter of this book briefly summarizes the 350-year history of Navajo weaving and then describes in more detail the contemporary setting for Navajo weaving. The lively 1980s are marked by a number of social, economic, and aesthetic trends that contribute to the current status of Navajo weaving as an art form; I discuss in particular the weavers' autonomy, eclecticism, and emphasis on process. I have divided the textiles in the Gloria F. Ross Collection into five groups based on their design sources. The glossary contains definitions for pertinent weaving terms, historical and contemporary rug styles, and selected Navajo words. I've included in the bibliography books and articles I recommend for further reading, as well as full references for sources I've cited in the text.

Today, the Gloria F. Ross Collection reflects the major weaving trends and traditions of the 1980s. It documents a vital craft during a decade in which emergent artists created expressions of their society, spirituality, patrons, and, perhaps most important, themselves. As the craft moves on, there will always be more to see and more to say. As one weaver notes,

> We are going forward. We're not going back [to the old ways of living]. Just like you [white people], we're not going back, we're following you. We want [our kids] to go to school so our kids will learn how [to get] higher educations.

On looms throughout the Navajo Reservation today there are many rugs that build on the pieces in this collection. New yarns, innovative tools, and stimulating ideas for imagery are explored by weavers every day. Finding a final cutoff point for the collection as it is presented here was a major challenge because Navajo weaving is a living art. The Ross collection, we hope, will continue to grow and reflect future changes in Navajo weaving.

Navajo sheep below Ganado Mesa

[1] The Navajo word for any white (Caucasian) person is *bilagáana*, apparently derived from the Spanish, *americano* (Young and Morgan 1980:221). I use the Navajo term throughout this book.

[2] Gloria F. Ross has also collaborated with Richard Anuszkiewicz, Milton Avery, Gene Davis, Stuart Davis, Paul Feeley, Helen Frankenthaler, Robert Goodnough, Adolph Gottlieb, Al Held, Hans Hofmann, Paul Jenkins, Alexander Liberman, Richard Lindner, Morris Louis, Conrad Marca-Relli, Larry Poons, Clifford Ross, Lucas Samaras, Richard Smith, and Ernest Trova.

[3] James Clifford notes, "The boundaries of art and science, the aesthetic and the anthropological, are not permanently fixed. Indeed anthropology and fine arts museums have recently shown signs of interpenetration" (1988:228). He has discussed at great length "the art-culture system" in which objects—art and artifacts—move within a matrix where classifications and relative values can be assigned and reassigned according to context and perspective. Navajo weaving provides a provocative example of the art/artifact system in action.

[4] The subject of ethnographic collecting and exhibit-making has attracted considerable scholarly attention over the past decade. I am able here to reflect on only a few aspects of these enterprises. The complex interplay among collectors, curators, and "the collected" is addressed provocatively and with much insight in such works as Ames (1986, 1992), Clifford (1988), Karp and Lavine (1991), Stocking (1985), and Vergo (1989).

[5] Recent writings on this subject challenge earlier notions of museum authority and examine issues of cultural representation. See, for example, Dominguez (1986), Jules-Rosette (1984, 1990), Karp *et al.* (1992), and Myers (1991).

[6] Several publications and exhibits authored and curated by Navajos already point the way. Ruth Roessel has written and edited a number of significant works about weaving (Roessel 1970, 1981, 1983). The periodicals *Tsá'ászi'* and *Diné Be'iina'* have provided outlets for articles written from the native perspective. *Navajo Weaving: From Spider Woman to Synthetic Rugs*, curated by Harry Walters, was mounted at Navajo Community College's Ned Hatathli Culture Center in 1977-78. Weaver D. Y. Begay is an active participant in planning a major catalog and exhibition of Navajo blankets and rugs at the National Museum of the American Indian, scheduled for 1994-95.

[7] Fear of witchcraft and other misfortunes eventually outweighed any possible advantages of "going public." Both weavers originally agreed to my using their names because their work had already appeared in several books and magazines—without their permission, however. Unfortunately, Navajo weavers often discover their work has been reproduced without permission although the U.S. copyright laws are intended to protect their creative products as they do all artists' works. The sale of a work of art does not automatically transfer copyrights to the buyer; the artist retains all copyright privileges, and the work may not be reproduced in any form without permission.

THE WEAVER'S WORLD

When you understand weaving, it's like being university educated. Good weaving
is an advanced study, when you know about all these rugs and how they are made.
It's like you start in the low grades and work your way up to the twelfth grade,
and then go to the university. As you weave each rug, you learn about your mistakes,
and you learn more each time. So, it means I'm like a college professor.

Rose Owens

More than anything else, contemporary Navajo weavers want others to know that they put concerted thought and hard work into their rugs and tapestries. They take weaving seriously, but without losing the good-natured humor that keeps life in balance. Their motivations are aesthetic and spiritual, as well as practical and economic. Many weavers feel strong links between their work and traditional Navajo culture, but they are no more interested in being slavish servants of the past than they are in being passive tools for innovations inspired by Anglo traders. Modern weavers defy the common stereotype of a lone Indian woman, always in native costume, herding her own sheep, shearing, carding, spinning, washing, and dyeing wool, handweaving a rug with a familiar "Navajo" pattern named after the local trading post, and mutely exchanging that rug at the post for groceries. In the late twentieth century, weavers have made increased commitments to high quality in their rugs and to successful marketing strategies. Their status as professionals and artists is growing. This is a story, or rather many stories entwined, about contemporary Navajo weavers and the emphasis they place on autonomy, eclectic innovation, and process-over-product in their thoughts and actions.

In conversations about weavers, Navajo people are always saying, "It's up to her." I hear this phrase when I'm traveling across the Navajo Reservation in northern Arizona and New Mexico, and I hear it when weavers visit my Phoenix home in central Arizona. They say it in Navajo, "*T'áá bee bóholníih*," and in English. When I ask what designs should be used in a rug, how big someone else's rug is going to be, or where another weaver might sell her work, the reply is invariably, "I don't know. That's up to her" or "That's how I do mine. I don't know how other ladies do theirs." I hear it especially when I ask what a rug pattern means or stands for: "Well, I couldn't say. It's up to that weaver."

This respect for the autonomy of others shows up in many facets of Navajo culture—in language structure, family relationships, and religious beliefs. No one should speak for another. To do so would be presumptuous and inappropriate, an invasion of privacy and personal privilege. Ideally, no one makes decisions for someone else, nor would anyone venture to predict someone else's opinions or plans, even those of a close relative. Each person must take responsibility for his or her own actions. One scholar calls this pervasive theme of respect for the individual "the primary ethical maxim" for Navajos (Farella 1984:193).

Throughout the 350-year evolution of Navajo weaving, the individual's freedom to make decisions—about color, design, or any of the myriad aspects of making a textile—has remained central. Outsiders often underestimate this autonomy in placing emphasis on the Pueblo, Spanish, and Anglo contributions of materials, techniques, and designs, on the commercial nature of Navajo weaving, and on traders and collectors, rather than on the weavers themselves as the spokespeople for the craft. Certainly, weavers make their decisions within the historical context of outside contacts and the cultural context of economic necessity. And, their choices are reinforced or limited by the marketplace, technology, and other external forces. Nevertheless, each weaver ultimately determines to what extent she will use or modify preceding styles or adopt new ones; she alone decides what her next rug will look and feel like and where she will sell it. Precisely because of the many outside influences and the frankly commercial nature of weaving, each weaver shapes her final product. In Navajo culture, after all, "It is up to her."

Many Navajo women weave, in part, because their mothers and grandmothers wove before them and they believe it is important knowledge for a woman to have: "Weaving is my life. It's something that was given to me by my mom."

A weaver in her fifties says, "This is how my mom taught me. Maybe she was taught by my great-great-grandmother. It's still with me, and I will teach my grandchildren." Weaving is an integral part of a woman's role in Navajo society and a culturally acceptable means of making a living. One weaver recalls, "My mother said to me, 'This is very important for you when you grow up.' She said that if a woman knows how to weave, she will always have plenty to eat, plenty of clothes, a good home."

Economic concerns are often paramount: "I usually weave a lot when [we need] kids' clothes, school stuff, and things like that." Another weaver explains, "I looked at my mom [who is a good weaver], and she could buy whatever she wanted, and that made me keep on weaving." A male weaver comments, "Weaving, it feeds me, it clothes me, it gives me mostly everything that I want." One young weaver has specific goals on her mind: "Weaving makes it so that I can afford to go to school. Right now it's paying off my school loans." An elderly weaver who supports her family bluntly

1. Classic sarape, 1840-1860. Denver Art Museum: Gift of Miss Moreland M'Pike. 1938.414

says, "You weave only if you don't have money. If you don't have money, you might weave in a hurry." Some Navajo women look to weaving as an appealing alternative to working outside the home because it allows them to control their own schedules: "You're on your own, putting in your own time. And the money's good, too." "I'd rather weave than go out and get a job," says one woman, while another comments, "It's nice to work at home because I don't need a babysitter."

Many talk about weaving as a means of creative expression; they challenge themselves with new designs or unusual techniques. Two weavers in their twenties speak enthusiastically about this aspect of their work: "I see weaving as an art, something I created on my own," and "I love it when a design goes through my mind." A male weaver says, "Weaving is part of art. Instead of holding the paintbrush, you use the yarn and wool." Another weaver compares her standards to those of successful architects: "All of us [in the family] are pretty good weavers. [We] do beautiful work. It's like in the Anglo world—the people who make buildings want to do nice work. It's the same thing [with weavers]."

Not all weavers work regularly throughout their lives, but understanding how to weave and affiliating with the larger community of craftspeople is important even to those who weave occasionally. Some give up weaving when they get married and begin raising a family or when they find a job outside the home: "I was weaving before I started to work at the boarding school, thirty years ago." Others only begin to weave after they become adults, perhaps after losing a job or after their children start school: "I was in my forties [when I started weaving], because my husband left me alone with the kids."

They may be motivated temporarily by income needs or by a fascination with their heritage, but their motivations change as other activities compete for time and interest. "I've got too much to do now. I do a lot of traveling. After I settle down, I'm going to be working with the wool again."

Only a few women place personal expression or cultural revival entirely above monetary reward. Some emphasize weaving as a special marker of Navajo ethnicity: "We [Navajos] were all born into weaving." A woman in her thirties says, "It would be a shame if the weaving got lost after all our mothers knew so much about it. [By weaving] I'm trying to keep the traditions." A small number save their handwoven goods for their family as heirlooms of their cultural and personal heritage: "My daughter is going to go on to college. I was thinking that I could weave her a little rug." Very rarely, someone talks of weaving as a hobby, a recreational activity without material rewards. A college student in her twenties says, "It's fun and keeps you busy. If you have nothing to do, you can weave." Another young woman wishes it *were* a hobby for her: "I wish I had another income. Then I would weave, and, instead of selling my rugs, I would decorate my own house."

For most Navajo weavers, their involvement in the process of weaving—thinking about designs, working with the wool, and spending long hours at the loom— equals or surpasses their interest in the final product, which is almost always sold as soon as it comes off the loom. Weavers talk eagerly about their dyes, spinning technique, and the minute details of weaving on an upright loom. They explain how particular motifs are constructed rather than what they symbolize. When describing the essential aspects of weaving, an arthritic seventy-year-old weaver, who no longer makes her own yarns, still emphasizes the origins and processing of materials: "The wool comes from our sheep. The most important thing we do is feed the sheep well and keep them [safe], card the wool and spin it. You have to think about the dye too."

Navajo weavers make frequent references to their thoughts and to the power of thought in the process of weaving: "I put a lot of thinking into [my weaving]. Even when I'm eating, even at night, I think about how I'm going to weave. My head and eyes are affected. Thinking about how I want to make [my rug] makes my head ache. I think about how nice the weaving will be." This is not just a matter of planning or worrying, but, in the Navajo way, it is willing the weaving process forward through the force of one's thoughts. While an eclectic mix of materials and ideas is actively sought from various sources, designs are consistently said to come from the mind: "I didn't use any [drawn] pattern. I just had it in my mind to put it in this way so the design would look better," says one who has been weaving for over sixty years. Another weaver describes her sense of absorption into the weaving process: "From head to toe, you are saturated with weaving. You are thinking, 'How am I going to design it?' Everything is put into weaving a rug. Then, your thinking is sold to an Anglo. It seems like you are selling your mind because you put so much into the rugs."

HISTORICAL BACKGROUND

The history of Navajo weaving is often divided into four major periods that coincide with major events in Navajo history: Classic, 1650 to 1865; Transition, 1865 to 1895; Rug, from 1895 to about 1950; and Recent, since 1950 (Kent 1985).[1] Although the rugs in the Gloria F. Ross Collection were all woven

between 1981 and 1992, knowing something of the earlier periods provides a foundation for understanding weavers today.

The Classic Period

The Classic period, 1650–1865, was a time of self-sufficiency and political autonomy for the Navajos. The tribe was loosely organized with dispersed, family-centered settlements across northern Arizona, northern New Mexico, and southern Utah. Having migrated from their Athabaskan homelands in Canada sometime after the fourteenth century, the Navajos were relative newcomers to the American Southwest, where Hopi, Zuni, and Rio Grande Pueblo people had been living in villages for many centuries. During the earliest part of this period, Navajos supported themselves through hunting and gathering, with sheepherding and small-scale farming added later. Kinship and clan networks dominated social relations. Athabaskan and Pueblo beliefs blended to form the rich assembly of origin stories and curing rituals that make up the Navajo religion today.

In this period, Navajos learned and perfected weaving techniques still used today. Scholars generally believe the Navajos learned loomweaving in the mid 1600s from their Pueblo neighbors, farmers with a long heritage of cotton growing and weaving. Navajo women most likely learned from weavers at Zuni Pueblo or from one of the western Rio Grande pueblos such as Jemez. Home-grown and home-processed materials, a limited range of colors, and simple banded and terraced designs mark the early blankets of this period. Spanish chronicles indicate that wool and cotton blanket weaving was well established among the Navajos by the early 1700s. Navajo textiles soon became an item of commerce in the active regional trade system. As time went on, Navajo weaving evolved. Plain

2. Germantown "eye-dazzler," 1890s. Denver Art Museum: Gift of Alfred I. Barton. 1954.413

stripes became elaborated with bold patterns of stepped triangles, blocks, and other geometric elements. Weavers incorporated motifs from their own basketry tradition, varied earlier Pueblo prototypes, and created new kinds of textiles as aesthetic and functional needs changed. The "chief" blankets and intricately patterned sarapes (fig. 1) of the Classic period were unique to the Navajos, with no precise counterparts elsewhere.

Ranging from thickly spun and coarsely woven utility blankets to extremely fine, even-textured "wearing" blankets with fancy patterning, Classic period textiles vary greatly in refinement. Classic weaving is also "characterized by a great deal of individuality, even idiosyncrasy . . . within the constraints of generalized design systems" (Brody 1976:6). Although we know little about individual weavers of this period, early records and subsequent ethnography suggest they were mostly women and worked at home, just as many do today.[2]

The Transition Period

Beginning in 1863, Navajo life changed radically. Many Navajos were forcibly held at Bosque Redondo in New Mexico to prevent their interference in Anglo-American westward expansion. Outside influences on their culture increased dramatically after their release in 1868. American settlers and the military moved onto their lands. The railroad crossed the Southwest in the early 1880s. Trading posts and Christian missions sprang up throughout the area. Travel and communication became easier. Wage labor and the availability of commercial goods led to the development of a cash economy. The government boarding school system brought unrelated children together and enforced new customs and values.

Navajos joined the consumer economy and experimented with entirely new resources and ways of life. Weavers used manufactured yarns and new dyes to develop styles such as the multicolored Germantown "eye dazzler" (fig. 2). They integrated into their work elements like serrated diamonds and vertical zigzags, borrowed from Spanish weavers of New Mexico's

3. Transitional rug, about 1900. Denver Art Museum: Gift of Anne Evans estate. 1941.286

Rio Grande Valley, where influences from earlier Saltillo weaving of northern Mexico had spread. Although they continued to incorporate older pattern elements, weavers began occasionally to substitute a center field surrounded by borders for a design field that traditionally extended from edge to edge of the fabric. As Navajo-woven floor rugs began to be sought after by a growing eastern market, weavers switched from making "wearing" blankets to rug production. This change, too, reflects the customary willingness of Navajo weavers "to change with the times. They have borrowed but have always integrated the new with the old, making it their own" (Wheat 1984:20).

The Rug Period

The first half of the twentieth century brought continued Navajo exposure to *bilagáana* customs and the development of modern reservation life. Government-imposed stock reduction programs, intended to preserve range land, instead brought trauma to a society centered on sheepherding. Formal education and jobs became tribal priorities. Nuclear families began to gain strength over extended families as the most significant household units. Subject to the bureaucracy of the Bureau of Indian Affairs and tribal government, dependent on a mixed economy with increasing wage labor, and drawn with other Americans into two world wars, the Navajos made major adjustments.

Nevertheless, the Navajo language was still used by many, even as English usage grew. Native religious practices continued. The Navajo Reservation remained predominantly rural. Many communities had no utilities, most roads were still unpaved, livestock and farming played a central role in the economy, and face-to-face interactions within small communities still ruled the day.

Women continued to weave in their homes and sell their rugs to local trading posts or craft stores, but weaving had become a commercial enterprise oriented almost exclusively toward the outside market system. Many families came to depend upon the income from weaving as a major part of their livelihood. With the occasional exception of saddle blankets and traditional two-piece dresses, few handwoven textiles remained in Navajo homes; rugs were now made "for external use only." Even as Navajo weaving became well known in national and international markets, weavers themselves were rarely noted by name, their rugs known only as works of an anonymous "Indian" or "Navajo" weaver.

Regional specialization developed during the Rug period. Often part of one large extended family or clan, weavers living in a single area developed similar, identifiable techniques and styles. Local traders rewarded certain features and made suggestions for further changes; a few initiated their own designs. Such traders worked closely with weavers to enhance the marketability of their rugs. New commercial yarns and packaged dyes, as well as a rising interest in home-brewed plant dyes, also sparked an increase in localized styles. Taking the names of communities or trading posts, early regional styles included Ganado, Klagetoh, Old Crystal, Two Grey Hills, Teec Nos Pos, Chinle, and Wide Ruins. Rugs of more general, less well-defined character were also woven in large numbers; one trader estimated that one quarter of the rugs woven in the 1950s belonged to no particular category (Maxwell 1963:52).

Throughout the reservation, rugs varied widely in technical quality, and many observers deplored the decline in nineteenth century standards of production. Regardless,

4. Early Crystal rug, 1900-1910. Denver Art Museum. 1928.28

excellent weavers continued to work, and many good examples of the craft survive from this period—a time in which the seeds of today's diversity were sown.[3]

The Recent Period

Since the 1950s, even as Navajo self-determination has risen, reservation life has grown increasingly to resemble that of surrounding Anglo-dominated areas. New housing, educational and medical facilities, and private businesses have developed. Civil rights efforts, including the American Indian Movement, have increased Navajos' pride in their ethnic heritage and raised serious questions about their economic dependency. With the Native American arts and crafts boom of the 1960s, many Navajo families discovered that the arts might hold a key to economic success.

Although many recent products from the loom are still called "rugs," many are destined for display on walls, and a new category, tapestries that are too thin and fragile for any use but decoration, has gained

popularity. The regional styles that developed during the Rug period continue to be made, but individual weavers' repertoires expand and styles slip the confines of geographic areas. Through publications, craft fairs, gallery promotions, and museum exhibits, weavers have become known by name, and collectors often seek out works by specific artists.

Always balancing between tradition and innovation, Navajo weaving of the Recent period remains a home-based, predominantly female occupation. But, tourism and commerce on the reservation and changes in family structure, women's roles, and job opportunities are prompting new trends. Weavers continue to reshape the craft. Increasingly they approach their work as professional artists. New materials, dyes, and designs prompt experimentation; galleries and independent entrepreneurs are replacing trading posts as principal buyers and sellers of rugs. Sophisticated design, production, and marketing systems are moving the craft into a new era of artistic and ethnic expression.

CONTEMPORARY SETTING & CULTURAL BACKGROUND

During the 1980s and early nineties, when the rugs and tapestries in the Gloria F. Ross Collection were created, Navajo life has been defined by an eclectic mix of traditional and modern. Solar panels spring up on log hogans. The seats of pickup trucks are covered with handwoven saddle blankets. Many Navajos are bilingual, some trilingual; they observe Christian and traditional Navajo religious practices simultaneously; they weave and hold down desk jobs. Many have mainstream American lifestyles, but strongly identify themselves as Navajo by maintaining ties with their extended families and honoring traditional beliefs and practices. One Navajo author writes,

> A Navajo woman can wear pants and yet believe and practice her culture to a far greater degree than another Navajo woman who does not believe and yet who wears Navajo clothes. Being a Navajo is not only something you see outside; also, it is something you feel and believe inside and in your heart (Roessel 1981:79-80).

With over 200,000 tribal members and nearly 24,500 square miles of reservation land in Arizona, New Mexico, and Utah, the Navajo Nation today is the largest American Indian group.[4] Administratively, the reservation is divided into 109 "chapters," community divisions functioning at a level somewhere between states and counties.[5] Chapter centers or "houses," often developed around trading posts, serve as meeting halls, conference centers, craft workshops, preschools, and laundromats. The tribal government has targeted six major and nine secondary "growth centers" for the development of shopping centers, grocery stores, theaters, restaurants, and other businesses.

Most of the reservation remains rural. Outside designated growth centers, small clusters of buildings with households of anywhere from two to twenty people are generally dispersed across the landscape.[6] Farm plots and grazing lands, allotted by the tribe to individuals but usually shared by the family, may be limited or extensive. Because many families continue to live in rural areas, many individuals commute long distances to in-town jobs. Electricity is only available in well-developed communities or along major thoroughfares. For many homes, water must be hauled from wells. Outdoor latrines are common.[7]

> Once when we went to Colorado, we saw mountains and still there were good highways and electricity that seemed [to come] out of nowhere. Here, it's just a flat area, and we can't even put in the electricity and running water!

Most rural home compounds are a conglomerate of disparate buildings.

A home site may include two to four houses, trailers, and/or hogans, each a primary residence for a nuclear family; an additional hogan for the grandparents, for ceremonial use, and for weaving; and a series of outbuildings, sheds, and corrals for work and storage. Hogans (traditional one-room, one-story, six- or eight-sided buildings) may be frame, block, log, or stone construction. Mobile homes and modern frame or block houses with multiple rooms for privacy are increasingly popular. Shacks made of assorted boards, packing crates, cardboard, and roofing tin still provide homes for many, despite government and tribal housing programs.

> Now there's a lot of things that make life more convenient. And we've left the hogan behind. . . . I was raised in a hogan made of branches. "Home pointed-together" it was called. We had a striped blanket hung in the doorway. When it snowed, the snow just came in.

Navajo society is organized principally around the women of a family: usually relatives on the mother's side of the family are considered closest, and inheritance passes along the female line.[8] The extended family—mother, father, and children, grandparents, aunts, uncles, their children and spouses—forms the core of most Navajo residence groups. A married couple generally expects to live near the wife's mother and her family if at all possible although many live elsewhere because of school, work, or personal preference. Family members who live together or nearby often share farming and livestock chores and transportation. With the support of hired specialists, the family organizes and conducts religious ceremonies and special events like weddings and funerals.

Membership in several of the more than sixty clans provides a means of establishing relationships outside the immediate family. Both women and men identify themselves as

Amy and Hanson Begay with their son, Northern Arizona University married-student housing, Flagstaff

belonging to their mother's clan and are said to be "born for" their father's clan. Traditional Navajo culture prohibits marriage between clan members. Formal introductions require the exchange of clan names.

Women in traditional Navajo society receive considerable respect and are property owners and decision makers. Women may serve as medicinewomen and participate at many levels in religious ceremonies. They are prominent as students and teachers, and they appear in the work force and in politics. Because rates of divorce, alcoholism, drug abuse, and family violence are similar to those in the off-reservation world, Navajo women face these contemporary pressures too. The Office of Navajo Women was established in 1978 by the tribal government to acknowledge and strengthen women's participation in tribal affairs and to reinforce their economic and social roles at home and in local communities.

Traditional Navajo religion, once central to all family activity, is now understood and practiced in varying degrees. In the 1940s, Navajos spent approximately one quarter of their time in traditional religious pursuits (Kluckhohn and Leighton 1974:225), but active participation today is considerably less.

In the traditional Navajo belief system, an elaborate set of origin stories and curing and preventative ceremonies lies at the heart of

keeping the universe in balance. Rather than following a regular, cyclical schedule like the Pueblos, Navajos arrange to have specialized medicine men or singers perform their complex ceremonies as needed. Navajos also perform shorter rituals, prayers, and songs ranging from girls' puberty ceremonies and house-blessing rites involving more than one family to personal acts of reverence such as a weaver's song when she takes a completed rug from the loom or a special blessing for a baby's first laugh.[9] Religion permeates the everyday values and actions of many people.

> The Old People didn't put their words down on paper; they just remembered everything—their origin stories, what they were told—all just by memory. To learn the stories, the young men and young ladies had to pay or trade, but my father told me about things—about the Holy People long ago, what they'd done, and about coyote stories. He led a good life. And now with my children, I am proud of myself for lecturing them and for the way my kids turned out. They're not running around. Some have their own homes, and they have cars and trucks.

Alongside traditional Navajo beliefs and practices, the Native American Church (the peyote cult) and various Christian denominations coexist on the reservation today (see Aberle 1982). Other religions, like the Baha'i faith, attract smaller, more isolated followings. It is not uncommon for Navajos to affiliate with several of these simultaneously.

Many households are moving away from the traditional subsistence economy founded on herding and farming. In 1974, the Navajo Office of Economic Development reported:

> As a result of rapid population growth on a fixed and deteriorating land base, there is no longer sufficient grazing lands to adequately support all of the Navajo people in their traditional manner. While over 65% of the Navajo people still live on land allocated them for grazing purposes, only 35% are employed in grazing activities in any full time effort receiving a reasonable return. (Navajo Tribe 1974:21-22).

Most Navajo families depend on several income sources, none of which, taken alone, would be entirely reliable. Seasonal and part-time jobs are more common than career positions and are often combined with farming, livestock maintenance, and other traditional activities such as craftwork and providing religious services.

Government jobs in the growth centers dominate the wage-labor market, and many women work at secretarial and clerical jobs or in service-oriented fields such as teaching and nursing. Women also hold most manufacturing jobs in the private sector, while men predominate in mining, construction, and commercial trades. Welfare and other government programs provide additional support to many needy families.

Noting that tourism produces considerable revenue, creates jobs, utilizes extant natural and cultural resources, and might additionally strengthen Navajos' views of their culture, the tribal government proposed a "Navajo Tourism Initiative" in 1988 that includes construction of new or upgraded resort motels and restaurants, visitor centers, a marina, and tribal park improvements (Navajo Nation 1988b:i-3). Undoubtedly, increased tourism will mean a growing market for Navajo rugs and other arts and crafts.

CONTEMPORARY WEAVERS

With the total Navajo population edging toward a quarter of a million people, there may be as many as 28,000 Navajo weavers today.[10] Traders, who watch the annual rug production closely, judge that there are as many as 8,000 to 10,000 weavers of excellent quality, with the rest producing rugs that range from very good to mediocre. No matter how they are counted, it is clear that there are many, many Navajo weavers.[11] And because Navajo

culture is built largely on personal freedom rather than explicit rules, a person can find many ways to be a weaver.

What sets weavers apart from their nonweaving relatives, friends, and neighbors is the knowledge and skills they command and the prestige and security these provide. This means not simply knowing how to spin a thread, but actually making something useful, something that earns a living and brings psychological and social rewards as well. In common with other craftspeople, ceremonial singers, and farmers, weavers earn their livelihood from special knowledge coupled with hands-on doing. Those who are successful work hard and are committed to making a living, while preserving a chosen lifestyle.

> I'll keep on weaving until I die!
>
> Sometimes I think if I didn't know how to weave, how would I be supporting my kids? Probably I'd be running around trying to get a job. But I'm glad I weave; it's not that hard to weave. It's like a gift. My grandfather, before he passed on, used to tell me to keep on weaving. He used to tell us to keep on doing it. He used to tell us that if you weave, you wouldn't starve. You always have something if you weave. It's just like looking forward to something all the time when you finish a rug.
>
> This is my life, it's been given to me from my mom, and from God. It's very, very important to me.

In real life, there is no "typical" Navajo weaver and no special class status that sets weavers apart. In their families and communities, weavers play the same roles as nonweaving women of similar age and experience. Their lifestyles vary widely—in family size and composition, educational background, religious beliefs and practices, economic concerns, and all the subtle differences that result from unique intersections of personal, historical, and cultural circumstances. Some weavers live comfortably within the confines of tradition, while others grapple with

new roles as artists acclaimed by the *bilagáana* world.

Many weavers speak Navajo and English interchangably. Some women, particularly the older generation, may speak only Navajo, while younger weavers sometimes speak English exclusively. Some speak Spanish as a third language. Overall, weavers have no more or less formal education than other Navajos, who average six and a half years of public schooling (Navajo Tribe 1980:9). Most adult weavers have had at least some elementary education, but many never attended school. Many younger women have finished high school and are attending or considering college classes.

> I went to school, but I didn't go very long. I just went to about sixth grade. But I used to color a lot in school, and I used to blend a lot of colors, and my teachers used to say, "Oh, that's pretty. Pretty colors in there." Now I use all different colors in my weaving.
>
> Weaving makes it so that I can afford to go [to college]. Right now it's paying off my school loans.

Children of most well-known weavers are completing their secondary school education more frequently than their parents. Although attainment levels for the general population have doubled during each decade since the 1940s, weavers' children appear more likely to finish high school and go on to college.[12] Compared to the average reservation resident, successful weavers have more disposable income and apparently give their children positive exposure to the outside world, including strong motivations for education.

Weavers depend heavily on their craft income, but in only a few cases are they sole providers in their households. Other family members commonly contribute through their livestock and small fields and through wage labor and salaries from jobs away from the home. Government welfare programs and seasonal and part-time activities like piñon-gathering also assist. Many weavers raise and maintain livestock; some, especially those who have "moved to town," keep livestock at relatives' homes, where someone else cares for them regularly. This mixed economy supports many families and allows weaving income, however large or small, to be an integral part of household finances.

> Weaving, that's all I do. I don't do any other work, ever since I started weaving. I'd rather weave than go out and get a job.

> With weaving, you can always get a little extra money. Since there are no good jobs to support me, my mom and dad said I'd better learn to weave.

Earnings from the sale of rugs may be sporadic and quite modest, as in the case of a weaver who makes rugs when her household needs groceries or gasoline money. Or, the income can be steady, as when a weaver pushes to make a rug every month in order to pay bills. Weavers who can afford the time and are willing to expend the effort it takes to produce a high quality rug can command large sums of money.[13]

> I think I make more out of weaving than working. You have to go back and forth [and buy gas]; you have to pay a babysitter, too. Comparing the price [of a rug] and the wage you get at a job, the work's kind of low. I get more in one time [by making a rug].

> I sell a rug every month because I have to pay my bills every month.

> I can make more money if I make a big rug. Those ladies who make little ones don't get as much even if they can finish their rugs real fast.

Like other Navajos, weavers have always lived in homes scattered widely across the Navajo landscape. Now, housing developments, along with shopping centers and other modern services, are being built in many of the Navajo Nation's growth centers, and some weavers are moving to these "suburban" locations. In addition to enjoying the year-round comforts of indoor plumbing and central heating, weavers with electric lights can

Evelyn, Robert Jr., and Brett Owens with Marvin Owens at his graduation from Central High School, Phoenix

continue to work after dark.[14] Looms may be put in a separate room, protected from children and household pets.

> If you weave in the hogan, [your rugs] won't be so straight. The hogan isn't so high to stretch your weave out, that's how [a rug] comes crooked sometimes.

Although the practice is becoming less common, some families still retain rights to land in a nearby mountain area, where their livestock is taken each summer. Some still move their households between their established winter home and a summer camp in the mountains. Weavers may haul their looms back and forth. Others stay in one place and hire a herder to take their flocks to summer grazing land, though they usually check on them each weekend.

> [My husband and sons] took the horses way up there in the mountain where there is some water. I stayed down here to weave.

Almost without exception, weavers and their families own at least one vehicle or have access to one. Weaving often finances at least part of the purchase and supplies gasoline money. Transportation has become a daily necessity for commuting to jobs, and weavers sometimes have to travel great distances in order to sell their rugs at the best price.

Most weavers have traveled away from the reservation—at least they have gone to a nearby city to shop, to visit family and friends, or to keep medical appointments. Many, especially those who demonstrate the craft for museums and galleries, have left the state and traveled to other parts of the country. Still, off-reservation travel is newsworthy business, the subject of many conversations and anecdotes, a good excuse to pull out snapshots. From these trips, weavers harvest new ideas for rug designs, new yarns or dyes, and new prospects for their rugs.

> I love to meet people. I know this lady and man from California. We took my mom and aunt to Salt River Canyon. This was on our way to Durango, Colorado. . . . And here's Brigham City, Utah. We went to visit these two couples. . . . We went to the University of Utah too. And this is Taos, New Mexico.

> They asked me to go to Minnesota to demonstrate my weaving, but I couldn't go. I've never been to the airport, and I didn't want to. I never traveled like that. I was scared to go. Sometimes you get lonely.

Those weavers who live off the reservation generally make trips back as often as they can afford to. For some, this means driving long distances almost every weekend to be with family, but it allows them to pick up weaving supplies, get advice and encouragement from other weavers, and sell their rugs to familiar traders.

Navajo weaving is now at an important juncture. Women can choose between weaving and many other activities to support, express, and entertain themselves. Those who consciously decide to weave are growing in number and strength, moving between many worlds, and balancing many roles.

[1] The earliest weaving after 1650 (for which there is documentary evidence, but no extant fabrics) should probably be considered a Pre-Classic or Formative phase of the Classic period, just as a separate Late Classic phase is sometimes noted from 1865 to 1885.

[2] I am greatly indebted to Joe Ben Wheat for information on the early history of Navajo weaving and the connections between Pueblo, Navajo, and Hispanic weaving (Wheat 1976, 1977, 1979, 1981, n.d.). Drawing on Wheat's original research, as well as her own, Kent (1985) also presents a clear and concise reconstruction of Navajo weaving history.

[3] Works that document the period include Bryan and Young (1940), Moore (1987), Newcomb (1964), Reichard (1934, 1936, 1939), and Rodee (1981).

[4] Sources for Navajo demographics include the Navajo Tribe's Overall Economic Development Program reports (Navajo Nation 1972, 1974, 1979, 1980), Eckert *et al.* (1989) and Faich (1981). The most recent population estimates, from 1988, range from 206,335 to 218,019, with approximately 20,000 to 30,000 of those living off the reservation (Eckert *et al.* 1989:19).

[5] For more on tribal government history and organization, see Wilkins (1987), Bingham and Bingham (1987, 1976), Iverson (1983), Eck (1982), Bailey (1980), and Young (1961).

[6] Households are comprised of those who eat and sleep together; residence groups consist of a number of households in close proximity "organized around a head mother, a sheep herd, a customary land-use area, and sometimes agricultural fields" (Witherspoon 1983:525).

[7] In 1974, 61% of Navajo homes had no electricity, and 80% were without plumbing (Navajo Tribe 1974:40).

[8] Precisely what form Navajo social organization takes is a major point of discussion among scholars. For more about the subject, see Aberle (1961, 1963), Shepardson and Hammond (1970), Lamphere (1977), and Witherspoon (1983).

[9] For further reading on traditional Navajo religion, see Reichard (1970), Gill (1981), Brugge and Frisbie (1982), Farella (1984), and the many publications of Father Berard Haile, Leland C. Wyman, and Karl W. Luckert.

[10] Estimates range widely, from as few as 12,000 (Hedlund, cited in *Sunset* 1987:106) to as many as 28,000 (Roessel 1983:596). The former was based on extrapolations from census records and demographic data, on informal surveys of rug outlets on and off the reservation, and on estimates made by several active traders. The latter was based upon a 1973 chapter-by-chapter survey sponsored by Navajo Community College that included all adult Navajo women who "knew how to weave." Getting a precise figure is complicated by the many ways to define a weaver (full- or part-time, knowledgeable or practicing, home consumption or market-oriented, and so forth). In my 1981 community study, roughly 40% of all women of appropriate ages were known to weave to any extent, from constantly to occasionally. Considering that this was a community chosen for study because of its many weavers, a reservation-wide estimate might well fall somewhere just under 30,000 total weavers. Traders, who have the opportunity to see more weavers than anyone else, suggest a range from 5,000 to 20,000. Clearly, a definitive survey with carefully planned sampling techniques would be extremely useful.

[11] It should be noted that, during the twentieth century, the number of weavers per capita has, however, dropped steadily, at least until the 1970s, when younger women began to take up the craft with increasing frequency.

[12] Almost half of the weavers represented in the Ross collection have children who have attended, or are currently attending, college. This is remarkable when compared to the relatively low total number of Navajo students in post-secondary education, 2,902 out of 10,000-20,000 of the right age in 1987 (Navajo Nation 1988:90).

[13] Average per capita income in 1980 was $2,414 (Navajo Tribe 1988:10). A well-known professional weaver can earn considerably more than this for a single rug, but most would have to weave many rugs to earn so much.

[14] Some weavers don't think weaving at night is a good idea even with electric lighting because they would be working too hard and upsetting the natural balance of life; others are willing to take the risk of pushing to excess and making errors (especially mismatching colors).

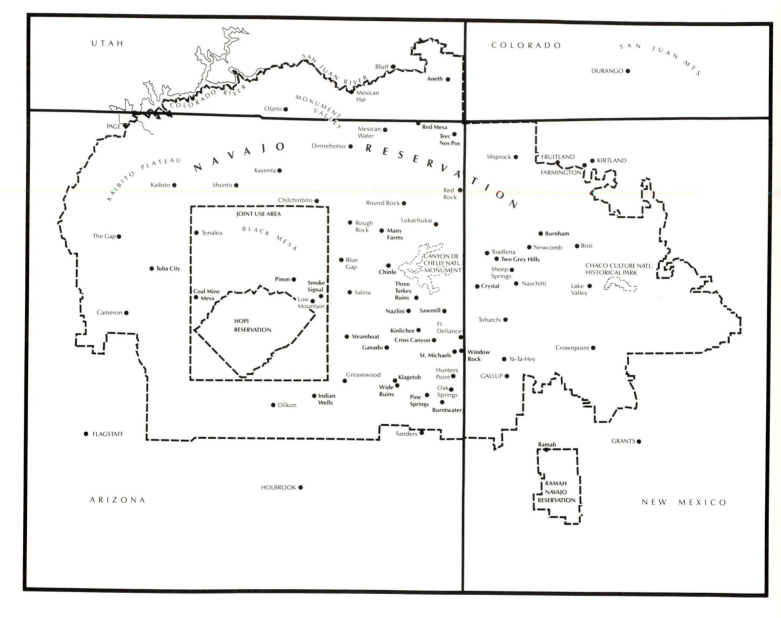

UTAH

COLORADO

SAN JUAN MTS.

DURANGO

SAN JUAN RIVER

Bluff
Aneth

Mexican Hat

MONUMENT VALLEY

Oljeto

PAGE

Mexican Water
Red Mesa
Teec Nos Pos

Dinnehotso

Shiprock
FRUITLAND
KIRTLAND
FARMINGTON

KAIBITO PLATEAU

NAVAJO

RESERVATION

Kaibito
Shonto
Kayenta

Red Rock

The Gap

Chilchinbito

JOINT USE AREA

BLACK MESA

Round Rock

Rough Rock
Lukachukai

Burnham

Tonalea

Many Farms

Toadlena
Newcomb
Bisti

Tuba City

Blue Gap

CANYON DE CHELLY NATL. MONUMENT

Two Grey Hills

CHACO CULTURE NATL. HISTORICAL PARK

Pinon
Smoke Signal

Chinle

Sheep Springs

Coal Mine Mesa

Low Mountain

Three Turkey Ruins

Crystal
Naschitti

Lake Valley

Salina

Cameron

HOPI RESERVATION

Nazlini
Sawmill

Tohatchi

Steamboat

Kinlichee
Cross Canyon

Ft. Defiance

Crownpoint

Ganado

Greasewood

Klagetoh

St. Michaels

Window Rock

Ya-Ta-Hey

Hunters Point

Wide Ruins

Oak Springs

GALLUP

Indian Wells

Dilkon

Pine Springs

Burntwater

FLAGSTAFF

Sanders

GRANTS

Ramah

HOLBROOK

RAMAH NAVAJO RESERVATION

ARIZONA

NEW MEXICO

THE GLORIA F. ROSS COLLECTION

Like any survey of a living, innovative art, the Gloria F. Ross Collection of Contemporary Navajo Weaving defies simplistic organization. Because Navajo weaving is eclectic, I've chosen to arrange the collection in a way that emphasizes the varied sources weavers draw on for inspiration. While reflecting the importance weavers themselves give their sources, this organizing principle also makes for a meaningful visual arrangement of the woven designs. At the same time, it allows us to see how individual weavers maintain a sense of identity while working within historically and culturally circumscribed situations and making textiles that will have commercial appeal. How a Navajo weaver goes about using the many stimulating design opportunities available to her is, after all, "up to her."

From this perspective, the weavers in the Ross collection may be divided into five somewhat arbitrary categories. Those in the first group carry on the legacy of earlier weavers by recreating nineteenth century blanket patterns and fulfilling commissions. Another group illustrates the evolution of Teec Nos Pos and Two Grey Hills, two regional rug styles that first appeared in the early twentieth century and have continued to develop parallel technical and aesthetic standards. Although some work within the framework of regionally defined styles and others consciously create their patterns de novo, eight weavers represented in the collection find their artistic "voices" through vegetal dyes. Yet another group focuses on pictorial images of the natural and supernatural worlds. Further attesting to the craft's diversity today, still another group actively experiments with shapes, textures, and functions.

Some explanation about the entries that follow may be helpful. The completeness of its documentation makes the Gloria F. Ross Collection of Contemporary Navajo Weaving especially valuable to experts. Pieces are documented with their dates and places of manufacture, makers' names, and relevant biographical and cultural information collected in the field. I've listed clan affiliations because the weavers themselves consider them a significant aspect of identity. I have assigned descriptive titles to works unless they had already been given a formal name by the weaver (indicated by italics). Even for the relatively new works in this collection, I've thought it important to include details of ownership and exhibition history because they can tell us much about the avenues for marketing that limit and, paradoxically, inspire the choices weavers make. These details of provenance are given in chronological order with the final acquisition made by the Denver Art Museum.

Because information about the textile's construction is of paramount interest to the weavers, I have appended a technical analysis to each entry. Experts will also find this information especially useful. The basic format I've used for technical data follows Kate Peck Kent's catalog for the Navajo textile collection of the School of American Research, *Navajo Weaving: Three Centuries of Change* (Kent 1985:116–130). Material sources represented in the Ross collection—raw and commercial fibers, yarns, and dyes—include most of those used by Navajo weavers since the late 1970s. Measurements are given in inches and in centimeters, with the length, as measured along the warps, always first. Only four pieces in the Ross collection were woven wider-than-long, that is, with the weft dimension larger than the warp dimension: Irene Clark's rug entitled *Nááts'íílid*, Grace Henderson Nez's chief blanket, Isabell John's pictorial, and the anonymous *yé'ii bicheii* weaver's tapestry rug. Standard notation is used for direction of spin, number of plies in a yarn, and direction of final twist in a multiple-ply yarn. Warp and weft counts are given as threads per inch. Photographs are usually oriented with the warp yarns in vertical position. I've noted as exceptions those cases in which the textile's design warrants a horizontal orientation of the warps.

IMPROVISATION
Adapting Motifs and Weaving Special Orders

Many Navajo weavers actively seek design ideas from outside sources. Sometimes old rug designs are adapted or copied, or motifs are rediscovered and reused. Sometimes weavers take suggestions from the traders who market their work or from customers who specify designs. Nevertheless, the weaver herself decides what to choose from these diverse sources and how to transform them to her own liking. Almost all Navajo weavers describe their designs as coming, ultimately, from their own minds.

Soon after the Navajos learned to weave from Pueblo Indians more than 300 years ago, they began to develop new forms and designs. At first, they decorated their blankets with indigenous Navajo basket motifs—stepped triangles, nested diamonds, crosses, and beaded bands (fig. 5). By the late nineteenth century, they had added serrated diamonds and bright new colors to the repertoire. Like their predecessors, modern weavers continue to draw on their historical and cultural roots for inspiration and designs.

Beginning in the 1880s, Navajo weavers in the northern Arizona community of Ganado became interested in weaving "special orders" and revivals of old-style blanket designs (fig. 6). Trader J. L. Hubbell and his successors at Hubbell Trading Post showed weavers examples of earlier textiles that clients liked, as well as Hubbell's own concepts for bordered, elaborately patterned floor rugs. In adopting these suggestions, weavers mixed and modified motifs to suit themselves. The rugs were widely admired and collected, and today's Ganado Red regional rug style eventually evolved.

At present, designs once used for garments and blankets are again in demand, but this time around they are woven in textiles created as wall hangings, floor covers, or upholstery for custom-made furniture. Weavers who copy, borrow from, or adapt old designs are not only responding to the marketplace, but also paying homage to their heritage and the resourcefulness and independence of earlier weavers. "These are our old-time, long-time-ago designs. I got my designs from my mom, and she got them from her mom, and probably before that from her mom." Indeed, most weavers learn from their mothers or other close female relatives, and designs and work habits may be passed along family lines.

Increasingly, weavers from all parts of the reservation borrow ideas from books and catalogs. "I have a big book; a gallery sent it to me," says a weaver who draws inspiration from textiles woven 100 years ago. Trading posts and stores carry copies of books and magazines with color plates especially for their weaving customers. Well-worn copies of rug books and *Arizona Highways* magazines are often stuck between

5. Late classic sarape, 1860s. Denver Art Museum. 1934.86

loom bars or tucked under a weaver's seat for easy reference. A weaver who uses illustrations from three magazines for inspiration is not likely to produce a rug that resembles any one of the three, but an original hybrid that incorporates ideas from them all.

"Special orders," as weavers and traders call commissioned work, are not restricted to replicating old-style blanket patterns. As long as a century ago, American traders, soldiers, and travelers specified other custom designs, including pictorials and business signs. Weavers still take such commissions, sometimes with reservation: "People want rugs. They'll order one, and then I'll weave it. It's hard to do, because they complain about the colors," comments an experienced older weaver. A young weaver says, "I only do two special orders each year. They pay, but they don't do much for me [creatively]." Others are more willing. One weaver said, "Working from a picture gives me time to think on my own. It's more calm." Another approached weaving a special order as a challenge: "I wanted to see how it would come out myself." The certainty of a purchaser is also appealing: "I can weave whatever pattern you want. When it's finished I will call you."

The Ross collection rugs woven by three generations of one Ganado family show the impact of the Hubbell Trading Post and the local preference for Classic period designs. Grace Henderson Nez (1) and Gloria Begay (3), grandmother and granddaughter, wove designs of their own invention based on nineteenth century blanket patterns. While working at Hubbell Trading Post, Nez's daughter, Mary Lee Begay (2), was commissioned to reproduce one of the turn-of-the-century rug studies that Hubbell used as illustrations of the designs he wanted.

6. Moki stripe blanket, about 1900. Denver Art Museum: Gift of Alfred I. Barton. 1954.395

Teresa Martine's rug (4), woven at Ramah, New Mexico, also clearly derives from nineteenth century blankets. Unprompted by local traders, Martine's efforts are part of a grassroots movement of the self-governed Ramah Navajo Weavers Association. Drawing on old-style dyes and motifs, Martine and other Ramah weavers seek to establish a brand new tradition based, in part, on blanket revivals. They visit museums and pore over books for inspiration.

Two sisters from another Ganado area family were also commissioned to create works now in the Ross collection. Elsie Wilson (5) was asked to make a rug in the contemporary Ganado Red style. She was given no instructions other than to make a Ganado Red rug in her own way. She jogged her memory with

scrapbook photos of her previous work and then developed a new plan in her mind, not on paper. Wilson's younger sister, Sadie Curtis (6), agreed to create a woven version of an image by contemporary painter Kenneth Noland for Gloria F. Ross Tapestries. Using the artist's colored pencil sketch as her model, Curtis reproduced it exactly.

Another Navajo/Noland was woven by Irene Clark (7) of Crystal, who incorporated her own vegetal-dyed colors and several commercial shades into the dramatic striped pattern, much as nineteenth century weavers often combined diverse raw materials in their striped blankets.

1

Grace Henderson Nez

b. 1913

Ganado, Arizona

Clans: *Ma'ii deeshgiizhnii* (coyote pass people), born for *Deeschii'nii* (start of the red streak people)

Grace Henderson Nez uses Ganado Red geometric patterns in designs from wearing blankets of past times. Like others who weave old-style designs today, Nez does so because they sell well, but she also feels a special relationship to them because they represent her family's patterns. "It was one of my mother's designs that she taught to me," she says of this rug.

And the family legacy continues. Nez taught her daughter, Mary Lee Begay, who in turn taught her two daughters and a daughter-in-law. These women all draw on the rich repertoire of historic Navajo designs that J. L. Hubbell urged weavers to copy, but they revise and recombine elements of it to suit their tastes. Unlike some mothers and daughters, Nez and Begay never collaborate on rugs; by keeping their projects separate, they keep their identities separate and, they say, keep peace in the family.

At 79, Grace Henderson Nez is one of the oldest weavers represented in the Ross collection. Like many Navajo women of her generation,

she speaks no English, wears traditional gathered skirts and jewelry, lives in a hogan, raises sheep, and exemplifies the Navajo values of hard work and even-tempered action. Until health problems limited her mobility, Nez maintained a summer sheep camp in the cool, mountain area known as Fluted Rock, in addition to her home at the base of Ganado Mesa. A grandson now lives with her and helps with household chores—a common support system in Navajo families.

A no-nonsense perfectionist, Grace Henderson Nez still works on a heavy, lumber loom her late husband built and painted turquoise-blue. It was already old when it was photographed in 1974 for an *Arizona Highways* special issue on Navajo weavers. She props up a large mirror behind the loom so she can see the back of rug as she works. Also visible in the mirror is the sparkling night skyline of Manhattan, a reflection of a poster hanging over her sofa—the urban world is not far away. Nez demonstrated weaving to tourists at Hubbell Trading Post during the seventies, and her family ties also give her important contacts with the outside world. One of her three sons, David Begay, completed graduate school and is currently assistant to the president for cultural research at Navajo Community College. Aiming at careers in computer science and with the airlines, two of her granddaughters have attended college in Phoenix.

Although she reminisces about the days when she used a variety of twill, double-faced, and sash-belt weaves, as well as tapestry weave, Nez now concentrates on bold, blocky designs that do not require the dexterity or keen eyesight needed for her finest earlier weaving. Even so, her work still displays the balanced appearance and consummate technique that comes from a long life of expert weaving. With a sparkle in her eye

and a shy smile, she says, "Weaving is good to me. I like it." This rug, a favorite design she has made many times, took her 2½ months to complete.

Woman's Chief-Blanket Style Rug
1988

Provenance: Acquired July 1988

1988.87

Dimensions: 119.0 x 137.5 cm. (46½ x 54 in.)

Tapestry weave, interlocked joins

Warp: handspun processed wool, z, natural white, 9/in.
Weft: processed wool yarn, z, aniline red, aniline black, aniline dark blue, aniline/natural blended light gray, 40/in.
Selvage cords: warp—commercial wool yarn, handplied, 2z-S, aniline brown, 2-strand twining; weft—commercial wool yarn, handplied, 2z-S, aniline brown, 3-strand twining

2

Mary Lee Begay

b. 1941

Ganado, Arizona

Clans: *Ma'ii deeshgiizhnii* (coyote pass people); born for *Kiyaa'áanii* (towering house people)

Gloria Ross commissioned Mary Lee Begay, a weaver employed by Hubbell Trading Post since 1971, to weave a rug with this particular design for the Denver Art Museum. The pattern comes directly from a small oil painting, a rug study done about 1905 by Bertha Little, a teacher at the Presbyterian College in Ganado. Trader J. L. Hubbell invited her and Chicago artists E. A. Burbank and H. G. Maratta, who also frequented the post between 1897 and 1909, to depict old-style Navajo textiles and his own modern adaptations in hopes of encouraging Navajo weavers to replicate them. Little made at least twenty-three such models. Today, trading post visitors can see dozens of the small paintings by Little, Burbank, and Maratta covering the "rug room" walls.

Although many weavers complain that copying a design verbatim is "boring" and not a productive use of one's mind, there is no known Navajo taboo against making duplicates. In this case, Begay copied

the design exactly as Little painted it, but she and other weavers often change motifs or colors to personalize the weaving. When weavers are taught, they are encouraged to tap their imaginations to create new designs, but copies and adaptations continue to be made. In fact, the traditional woman's dress (*bííl*) is always made of two identical panels, and many examples of duplicate rugs exist.

For this rug, Begay took several weeks just to spin the yarn from pre-dyed, commercially processed wool. After she began weaving on July 1, 1981, she worked thirty-six hours a week, and by July 28, the rug was half finished. The second half was completed over the next three weeks. Begay painstakingly wove the final two inches, first with a long umbrella rib and then a darning needle, in seven hours on August 15. Total weaving time amounted to about 200 hours, for an average rate of seventeen square inches per hour. This means the weaver advanced roughly one-third of an inch across the rug's entire four-foot width during an hour. After she removed the rug from the loom, she spent a final hour in brushing its surface to remove dust and lint and in knotting and trimming the corner tassels.

Proficient and versatile, Begay weaves at home as well as at Hubbell Trading Post. Although Ganado Red and Hubbell revival styles are her usual choices, she also makes Burntwater, Two Grey Hills, Storm, Wide Ruins, and many other patterns. Because she excels in designing, her work is often copied by other weavers.

Mary Lee Begay's life seems full of contrasts. Although she speaks little English, she is confronted daily by inquisitive tourists at Hubbell Trading Post, where she demonstrates weaving. Although her mother, Grace Henderson Nez (1), is a traditional weaver, Begay herself regularly receives commissions for innovative

contemporary tapestries and shows in urban art galleries. Begay's family raises cattle, sheep, and goats, which they take to their mountain camp each summer. Her brother is a college administrator, her two daughters study high-tech subjects in college, and one of her three sons is an urban sheet-metal worker. For her job at the post, she dresses in old-style Navajo garb—a multitiered broomstick skirt of satin or calico, a long-sleeved velveteen or satin blouse, and silver and turquoise jewelry, but she wears modern slacks and knit tops for her household and farmyard chores. Mary, her husband, and her brother instruct their children in traditional Navajo ways—arranging for religious ceremonies, for instance—even as they encourage the kids to complete their formal education and join the outside work force.

Begay began teaching her daughters, Lenah and Gloria, to weave when they were ten and eleven years old (3). She set up small looms and guided them through the whole process. After they finished their first simple, striped rugs, each girl was responsible for choosing her own designs. Even now that Lenah and Gloria are in their twenties, Begay still sets up their looms. In recent years, Begay also taught her daughter-in-law, Margaret, whose own mother does not weave.

A deeply spiritual person, Begay nevertheless approaches weaving pragmatically. Summing up her work, she explains in Navajo, "Weaving takes a lot of hard thinking. It's all I think about when I'm working. It takes careful measuring too. When you set up the loom, you must measure carefully to the middle. And you must measure over and over again as you put in the patterns so that they come out even. If it doesn't come out right, you take it out and measure again. And the sides, you have to count the side cords carefully too. I don't make my rugs cheaply—a lot of hard work is involved."

Hubbell Revival Rug 1981

Provenance: Hubbell Trading Post, Ganado, Arizona; acquired August 1981

1981.113

Dimensions: 180.0 x 120.5 cm. (71 x 47 in.)

Tapestry weave, interlocked joins

Warp: handspun processed wool, z, natural white, 9/in.
Weft: handspun processed wool, z, dark aniline red, aniline black, natural white, 36-42/in.
Selvage cords: handspun processed wool, 2z-S, dark aniline red, 3-strand twining

Bertha Little rug study

3

Gloria Begay

b. 1970

Ganado, Arizona

Clans: *Ma'ii deeshgiizhnii* (coyote pass people); born for *Tó dích'ii'nii* (bitter water people)

Using leftover yarns from one of her mother's projects, Gloria Begay worked on weaving this, her fifth rug, each day after returning from summer school classes at Navajo Community College. It took three months to finish. The rug's texture is even and the design well executed, but the marks of a beginner show in sides that are not perfectly straight. Begay vows to do better next time. With a mother and grandmother (2, 1) known for their superb weaving, her goals are high and the search for independence challenging. "My mom is an artist. I'd better keep weaving so that I can compete," she says. "My rug is going to be in a museum, and it's only my fifth. I'm proud, very proud. Oh wow! I'm an artist already, too. Watch out!"

The alternating black and blue stripes of nineteenth century "Moki" striped blankets (fig. 6) inspired her background pattern, one of her mother's favorites too. The young weaver found that, because of the concentric placement of colors, the nine square motifs were more difficult to weave than she had expected. She also joked that they began looking like "octopus suckers" to her. Part-way through, she was tempted to stop because the design looked odd, but her mother urged her to continue and not to make fun of her work. For traditional Navajos, weaving is a serious undertaking that should not be joked about.

Begay is working on an associate of arts degree in computer science at Scottsdale Community College near Phoenix. The money she earned from the Ross collection rug paid the first month's rent on her city apartment. Active in the campus Native American Club, she wore the crown of Miss Indian Scottsdale Community College during 1991 and attended Indian powwows and other events as part of her duties. She also works part-time in a Scottsdale gift shop and has held a variety of other jobs while going to school. She hopes eventually to earn a B.A. degree and go on for graduate training.

"I even want to go beyond the master's degree. I want to go to the limits. There are a lot of Navajos who graduate from high school and go to junior college or university, but they drop out. There are not so many Navajos that finish. Wouldn't it be boring to be out of school? If I weren't in school, I'd probably go crazy. Education is important for getting a good job, experience, and the means to educate others. The cost of college is high, and you have to sacrifice so much of your money, but I want my education to help me find a job."

While she lives in the Phoenix metropolitan area during the school year, she returns often to the reservation on weekends. She contemplates the historical and philosophical differences between the worlds in which she lives: "In my tradition, people say weaving was taught by Spider Woman. But through studies, you learn it was picked up from the Pueblo Indians. . . . When I took classes in Navajo culture and world history and geography, they said we came from the Athabaskans . . . . The Navajos emerged from Asia and came across the Bering Strait, and here we are today. But according to my uncle in the Department of Dine'e Studies at Navajo Community College, that's not true. And a scientist believes the sun comes up and goes down because the earth rotates. Well, to the Navajos, the sun comes up, and it's a god, and the earth is our Mother Earth."

Looking ahead to her future prospects for weaving, she notes, "I'm so busy, I'm afraid I won't even have time to weave. During my first year in college, my mother set up a loom for me, and I had confidence that I'd finish. But when school started and work began, that loom just sat in my closet. Finally my mother finished the rug. I only wove four or five inches."

For Begay, weaving may become secondary to another career. Nevertheless, it is clear that she carries on her mother's and grandmother's legacy. No one will be surprised if she is one day teaching her own daughters to weave.

Moki Stripe Rug 1991

Provenance: Acquired August 1991

1991.742

Dimensions: 92.0 x 62.0 cm. (36 x 24½ in.)

Tapestry weave, interlocked joins

Warp: processed wool yarn, z, natural white, 9/in.
Weft: processed wool yarn, z, natural white and pre-dyed aniline red, blue, black, 36/in.
Selvage cords: warp—processed wool yarn, handplied, 2z-S, 3-strand twining; weft—outer warps are processed wool yarn, handplied, 2z-S, aniline black, no twining

4

Teresa Martine

b. 1920

Ramah, New Mexico

Clans: *Chishi dine'é* (Mescalero Apache people); born for *Tó dích'íi'nii* (bitter water people)

With its muted colors, blocky meanders, and concentric rectangles, Teresa Martine's design is nearly identical to a blanket at the Field Museum of Natural History in Chicago (Kahlenberg and Berlant 1972:75), except that hers has five rectangles running across the middle and ends, and the earlier piece has only three. The Field Museum's blanket—an eye dazzler—was made with brilliant red, purple, and green aniline-dyed yarns that have since run and faded. Martine's version is subtly colored with the vegetal dyes she learned about in a workshop organized by the Ramah Navajo Weavers Association.

The Ramah Navajo Reservation, a small group of rural Navajo communities in west-central New Mexico, is separated geographically and culturally from the "Big Reservation." Because people living there often feel out of touch with mainstream Navajo life and especially with economic opportunities, the Navajo Weavers Association was founded in 1984 by seventeen traditional weavers with the help of a professional community planner. Their aims are to rebuild their community's economic base and to work toward renewed family and community self-reliance (mimeograph 1/18/85:1-2).

The association has introduced the *churro*, an old-style Navajo breed, and other specialty sheep into local flocks to improve wool quality, established a marketing cooperative for weavers, and initiated workshops and programs where women can refine their weaving knowledge. Every August, members exhibit and sell their work at Indian Market in Santa Fe. They have also created a line of handwoven pillow covers marketed through major department stores.

In the late 1980s, Teresa Martine and others studied imported and local dyestuffs through workshops taught by D. Y. Begay, a successful young weaver from Salina Springs on the "Big Reservation." The black, white, and gray in Martine's rug are natural sheep-wool colors. The blues come from various baths of Mexican indigo. The burgundy and peach are both dyed with brazilwood (*Caesalpinia brasiliensis*), which was used in the nineteenth and early twentieth century Hispanic blankets made in New Mexico (Bowen and Spillman 1979:208-209; Saltzman and Fisher 1979:213-214). The beige is a local lichen dye, and the tan is from cedar wood chips.

The nubby yarn that Martine carded and spun by hand for this rug shows the rough quality of some wool that weavers must contend with in Navajo country. Ramah weavers have been especially supportive of Utah State University's "Save the Churro" program that aims to reintroduce churro sheep, whose many-colored wool is smooth and silky. Weavers like Martine have acquired a number of excellent churros for breeding. Her own flock contains sheep with beautiful natural red-brown, brown, and black fleeces, but until the transition to full-blooded churros is fully in effect, she must choose her raw materials carefully.

Martine's mother taught her to weave at twelve. During the eighties Martine taught weaving through her chapter's Adult Education Program. Because she now cares for a handicapped son, she prefers to weave and spin at home. She enjoys making twill and two-faced rugs and sash belts, as well as tapestry-weave rugs inspired by old blankets she sees in books and magazines. Though now clouded with cataracts, her eyes light up with pleasure as she pores over pictures of rugs.

Martine's weaving provides essential income for her family's food and health care. She has twelve children, nineteen grandchildren, and seven great-grandchildren. Her mother, Luna Jake, is still living today, at the age of 109. Martine's husband works as a bus driver and is the pastor of the Full Gospel Church next to their home. Their quadriplegic son Calvin is a talented painter who must hold the brush in his mouth and needs many months to complete a single photorealistic work. For a time, the family lived in a housing development with electricity and plumbing in Pine Hill on the Ramah Navajo Reservation. When their expenses grew too great, they moved to the church grounds between Pine Hill and Mountain View, where their woodstove-heated house has no electricity or running water.

Martine's work allows her to continue a self-sufficient, family-oriented, sheep-raising way of life. By working at home, Martine is able to be there for her son, her husband, and their livestock, but she often speaks of teaching others to weave. She stays in touch with area women with similar interests through meetings and workshops of the weavers association.

Sarape Revival Rug 1988

Provenance: Ramah Navajo Weavers Association, Ramah, New Mexico, 1988; acquired at Indian Market, Santa Fe, August 1989

1989.120

Dimensions: 146.5 x 74.0 cm. (58 x 29 in.)

Tapestry weave, dovetailed joins

Warp: handspun wool, z, natural gray, 5/in.
Weft: handspun wool, z, natural and vegetal colors, 32/in.
Selvage cords: warp—handspun wool, orange, 2z-S, 2-strand twining; weft—processed wool yarn, 2z-S, gray, 2-strand twining

5

Elsie Jim Wilson

b. 1924

Kinlichee, Arizona

Clans: *Ma'ii deeshgiizhnii* (coyote pass people); born for *Deeschii'nii* (start of the red streak people)

Elsie Wilson lives eight miles east of Ganado, in the community of Kinlichee. There, many weavers make versions of the Ganado Red regional style, which usually consists of a central diamond (or double diamond) and fancy borders. The style originated early in this century when Ganado area weavers adopted trader J. L. Hubbell's suggestion to create predominantly red rugs with bold geometric motifs and simple borders. Today, main motifs are intricately elaborated with many smaller figures, background space is filled, and borders are fancy and multiple.

Although Wilson describes the rug as a Ganado Red, some might classify it as Klagetoh style because of its color balance. Named for a community about fourteen miles south of Ganado, Klagetoh rugs have design elements similar to Ganado Reds, but with gray centers and red backgrounds rather than the reverse. Such distinctions are often debated, and individual textiles often defy easy categorization. To Wilson, the classification doesn't really matter; she knows where she's from, and she weaves what she likes.

In Wilson's rugs, finely stepped motifs are typically repeated in central, filler, and border areas, creating complex positive/negative relationships. She frequently uses hooked frets and small stepped triangles. In this rug, the alternation of red and gray-brown concentric diamonds and surrounding panels gives the illusion of multiple layers.

To maintain maximum control and efficiency, Wilson uses a very unusual welded steel loom with a revolving upper beam onto which she rolls her warps; the beam is held in place with an adjustable ratchet to control the warp tension precisely.

Wilson is the eldest of three sisters who are all excellent weavers, each with a distinct style. Wilson's best-known rugs are her Ganado Reds, although she has worked with subtle vegetal dyes too. The middle sister, Sadie Curtis (6), was influenced in her designs while working at Hubbell Trading Post during the 1970s and makes chief-blanket style rugs, other revival patterns, and novelties such as American flag rugs. Until recent health problems, the youngest sister, Mae Jim, specialized in large Ganado Red rugs but also wove in other styles that caught her imagination, including Two Grey Hills and Wide Ruins. The sisters occasionally pair off to weave together, but professional rivalries usually keep them apart.

Wilson has three daughters and one son. She taught the two younger daughters, Ruth and Ruby, to weave after they had young children of their own and had worked outside the home for several years. The fact that her eldest daughter, Minnie, who does not weave, received a B.A. from Northern Arizona University in 1990 is a source of pride to Wilson because she didn't complete school and go to college herself. After third grade, her parents kept her at home to care for the livestock; that is when she learned to weave. When she was eighteen, her parents arranged her marriage in the traditional Navajo way, consulting with the boy's parents before telling her. She and her husband, Everett, have always lived at Kinlichee in a compound with several stone and stucco houses, a traditional hogan, a workshop/carport, and a large, well-tended garden.

As she has grown older, Wilson's physical strength and ability to manage the fine, large-scale weaving of her youth have waned, though her inner vision for rug designs remains acute. Ruby, her youngest daughter, often shares the most difficult tasks of stringing the loom and completing the final weft passages. "If it's something small," says Ruby, "we do it separately. Most of the big ones we do together. Usually I do the last part; that's where I come in. It seems like I do the hard parts, hard for her at her age. It's hard for her to see. Mostly it's her design and her thinking, and I just follow along."

In recognition of her efforts "to further Native American cultures," Elsie Wilson was one of four Native American artists to receive the 1990 Arizona Indian Living Treasure Award.

Ganado Red Rug 1982

Provenance: Acquired February 1982

1982.7

Dimensions: 149.0 x 93.5 cm. (59 x 37 in.)

Tapestry weave, interlocked and dovetailed joins

Warp: handspun wool, z, brown-white, 10/in.
Weft: handspun processed wool, z, natural blended brown, natural blended gray-brown, dark aniline red, natural white, 42/in.
Selvage cords: handspun wool, 3z-S, dark aniline red, 2-strand twining

6

Sadie Curtis

b. 1930

Kinlichee, Arizona

Clans: *Ma'ii deeshgiizhnii* (coyote pass people); born for *Deeschii'nii* (start of the red streak people)

This weaving is truly a meld of different worlds. Woven by Sadie Curtis, it was designed by contemporary American painter Kenneth Noland and commissioned by Gloria Ross. Titled *Reflection*, it is one of a series of such works that now hang in corporate offices, private homes, and public galleries in the United States, Europe, and Japan.

Gloria Ross contracted with the Ganado-area weaver to make *Reflection* in July 1983. At first, the white in the center rectangle bothered Curtis because it was different from the gray used in the other eight. She suggested they all be made the same, saying simply that they would "look better." Although Ross and Noland agreed to change the center color to gray, Curtis went back to Noland's original plan during the weaving process, which took about three months.[1]

Sadie Curtis is one of the most masterful weavers around. For years,

she worked as a craft demonstrator at Hubbell Trading Post. That was the time, she says, when she really learned to speak English, for she never completed grade school. Now retired from Hubbell, she works steadily on her looms at home and occasionally collaborates with her aunt, Alice Belone, another accomplished weaver. Curtis performed professionally for several years with a traditional singing group, "Kinlichee Maiden Singers," and often plays a tape of theirs while weaving in the hogan she and her husband share. Her sisters, expert weavers Elsie Wilson and Mae Jim, live nearby. Her only daughter, now in her thirties, has been weaving off and on for about two years, and two daughters-in-law have started learning. A young granddaughter showed enough interest that Curtis set up a little loom for her one summer in the late eighties.

Curtis's favorites are chief blankets and revivals of early styles, into which she integrates ideas from many sources—magazines, books, Hubbell's "little paintings" of nineteenth century wearing blankets, and other textiles. Like the rugs by her sister Elsie Wilson, Curtis's work often involves complex positive and negative relationships, with seemingly layered figures that appear to advance and retreat. In addition, she successfully experiments with Burntwater and other far-flung regional styles. She is especially proud of an American flag rug that appeared on the cover of *Arizona Highways* in July 1976.

Reflecting the prosperity they enjoy from their hard work, Sadie and Jack Curtis have a handsome home compound of both modern and traditional buildings surrounded by a well-kept garden and cornfields. Earl, a self-employed silversmith and leatherworker, is the only one of their seven children who has followed his mother into full-time craftwork. Curtis's daughter, June,

who works in a tribal office in Fort Defiance near Window Rock, occasionally weaves. Four of Curtis's sons went to school in Utah and, like many Navajo children, spent their growing-up years with *bilagáana* Mormon families. One of them, Emerson, now attends college there while the others are employed in Arizona, Utah, and Colorado.

Often laughing and joking while working at her loom, Curtis commented on *Reflection* in her typically laconic style: "It's pretty, but I don't know why. It wasn't hard to weave. In fact, it was easy. I hate making such big ones though; it takes a long time. A little one takes five days—easy money!"

[1] To some Navajo viewers these bicolored rectangles may appear to be similar in form to "rainbow lines" or "sundogs," motifs representing segments of rainbowlike prisms or beams of light that are seen through clouds around the sun (Reichard 1950:191). Usually red and blue, outlined in white, these motifs are traditionally used in ceremonial sandpaintings as signs of protection and supernatural conveyance. Curtis's only comment on the Noland rectangles was that they were "pretty."

Kenneth Noland *maquette*

Reflection 1983

Provenance: Commissioned by Gloria F. Ross Tapestries, New York, New York, 1983; acquired 1990

Exhibitions: *Kenneth Noland and the Navajo Weavers: The Ross Tapestries*, Gallery 10, Scottsdale, Arizona, March 1984

1990.164

Dimensions: 125.0 x 149.0 cm. (49 x 59 in.)

Tapestry weave, interlocked joins

Warp: handspun processed wool, z, natural white, 10/in.
Weft: handspun processed wool, z, aniline top-dyed black, blended gray-brown, dark brown, natural white, aniline red, 48/in.
Selvage cords: handspun processed wool, 3z-S, gray, z- and 3-strand twining

7

Irene Clark

b. 1934

Crystal, New Mexico

Clans: *Tábaahá* (water's edge people); born for *Honágáahnii* (he walks around one people)

In August 1990, Gloria F. Ross commissioned Irene Clark to weave this large tapestry design by Kenneth Noland. Because of its size, Clark's husband and sons built an extension on her loom. She prepared several dyebaths combining a native ground lichen (*ni'hadláád*) and "Navajo tea" (*ch'il gohwéhé, Thelesperma gracile*) to make the gold, orange, and brown colors. She purchased commercial yarns for the other colors, including two shades of green and a light blue-gray. Once the weaving began, "It was no different than the other ones I make," Clark says. "In fact it was kind of easy. The only thing was that I had to weave all the way across. It was so wide— eight feet long! I have a very wide bench that I sit on. When I was finished, I was tired, but that always goes away." She was obviously pleased with the rug's reception.

"Most of my sisters and kids saw it. They said it was real beautiful, different. They wanted to know what kind of lady wanted this rug. We used to talk about how there are all different kinds of people, different ways of thinking, different tastes in this world. I think it was an exciting rug to make, even though it was sort of plain. While I was weaving, I thought about a rainbow, and we gave it a name that means 'rainbow' in our language. I also thought about the Navajo blankets that they used to make—the chief blankets. With its stripes going across, not standing up, it was like that old kind of blanket."

As she made *Nááts'íílid*, Irene Clark personalized and emphasized its Navajo nature through her weaving technique. She interpreted the striated lines of Noland's drawing with subtle pinstripes known as "wavy lines," an effect that typifies weaving from the Crystal area where she lives.

Several months after the completed rug was sent to New York, Gloria Ross received a note that further underscored the "Navajo-ness" of the commissioned work. It was written by Irene Clark and her son, Ferlin, a Harvard graduate student: "Upon your request to name the rug you bought from me, I had to take some time to think what it means to me. Usually, Navajo rugs are not given a name but are distinguished according to geographic location. . . . I am proud of the rug I wove and sent to you. Proud, because this rug symbolizes the strength of my family. Every strand of naturally dyed yarn interwoven is my family's clanship and the belonging to one another. All the colors of the rug symbolize the array of colors depicted in the rainbow. The rainbow is a strength that protects and paves the path to beauty and harmony. As a nation, the Navajo people and our government continue to be protected by the rainbow. The rainbow also signifies sovereignty.

. . . Our rich culture, our dynamic clanship, and our authentic language are genuinely Navajo, and so is the rug you have now. Thus, I have named the rug *Nááts'íílid*."

Kenneth Noland *maquette*

Nááts'íílid (**Rainbow**) 1990

Provenance: Commissioned by
Gloria F. Ross Tapestries, New York,
New York, 1990; gift of Gloria F.
Ross and Kenneth Noland, 1992

1992.133

Dimensions: 124 x 251 in.

Weft-faced plain weave

Warp: handspun processed wool, z,
natural white, 11/in.
Weft: processed wool yarn, z, natural,
vegetal and aniline dyed colors, 52-60/in.
Selvage cords: processed wool yarn,
handplied, 2z-S, gray, 3-strand twining

By the early twentieth century, traders began to recognize and reinforce distinctive designs and color schemes shared by weavers in the same extended families, clans, and communities. These regional styles and a few other recognizable types constituted a quarter of all rug production in the 1950s and early 1960s (Maxwell 1984:53). The percentage was considerably higher by the 1970s, partly because magazines and books, like Maxwell's *Navajo Rugs—Past, Present, and Future*, gave weavers handy reference to the popular styles they defined and illustrated. Today, the percentage of weavers using recognized regional styles may be greater still.

As individuals move away from their extended families and their marketing resources expand, strict regional designations are breaking up. Even though *bilagáana* writers have identified between nine and nineteen styles across the reservation (Hedlund 1983:215), weavers rarely recognize by name more than a few styles other than their own. Paying little attention to artificial boundaries, weavers readily adopt and adapt any style they are attracted to. The textiles in this section represent the development and diversification of two regional styles, Teec Nos Pos and Two Grey Hills.

7. Two Grey Hills rug, Daisy Tauglechee, 1948. Denver Art Museum. 1948.445

Weavers around Teec Nos Pos ("Ring of Cottonwoods") and Red Mesa have made rugs in two distinctive styles since the turn of the century. Both take the Teec Nos Pos name and are characterized by jewel-toned, aniline colors balanced by dark or neutral shades of natural colors. One, also known as the "Red Mesa Outline" style, is marked by an all-over pattern of serrate-edged zigzags finely outlined in contrasting colors. Clearly derived from nineteenth century Germantown eye-dazzler blankets (fig. 2), the style is represented in the Ross collection by Mamie Begay's rug (9).

The second Teec Nos Pos type, represented by Bessie Lee's rug (8), has large geometric figures, often with hooked or fretted appendages, arranged on a central rectangular panel and surrounded by wide, patterned borders. Occasionally called "Thunder Trail" (although the name's origin is unknown), this style clearly springs from the bordered geometric patterns that developed when local traders introduced Oriental carpets to the Crystal and Two Grey Hills communities.

Despite their complexity, both styles, which have changed little in the decades since they originated, are still made by Teec Nos Pos weavers. "It's hard for me to make any other designs," says one weaver. "Even though it looks difficult, this one's easy because I already know it."

In the past few years, weavers outside the Teec Nos Pos area have begun to take the Teec style down new by-paths. Larry Yazzie (38) and his family from Tuba City and Coal Mine Mesa are exploring variations of the style because, he says, "It's got a lot of design in it. I start with the regular Teec Nos Pos designs like I find in the books. Then I change them around until they look nice to me. I keep interchanging the designs and mixing the colors."

In the early 1900s, Two Grey Hills area traders Ed Davies and George Bloomfield recognized the character and quality of the local weavers' work. They accepted the weavers' established aesthetics—such as their dislike of red—and counseled them to refine and elaborate the simple geometric patterns they were then making (McNitt 1962:260). Weavers freely borrowed ideas from neighboring areas such as Crystal, New Mexico, where frets, hooks, and other Oriental carpet motifs had been adopted, but they also explored patterns based on their own imaginations. By the mid 1920s, they had established the Two Grey Hills style, typified by symmetrical, geometric patterns of right-angled, bordered motifs woven with thin, closely packed yarns of natural and blended grays, browns, white, and top-dyed black. During the late 1940s, Daisy Tauglechee's refined imagery and technical control brought the region widespread acclaim (fig. 7). More than any other Navajo rug style, Two Grey Hills has captured the attention of weavers and buyers alike. Selling for $60,000, a Two Grey Hills rug set a record price for contemporary Navajo weaving in 1987. The style is often the only one tourists have heard about.

The Ross collection rug by quintessential Two Grey Hills weaver Daisy Tauglechee (10) exemplifies the style, while three other pieces show individual variations. Barbara Jean Teller Ornelas (11) pushes Tauglechee's high standards of excellence even further with higher thread counts, exquisite spinning, and even more intricate motifs. Bessie Barber (12) and her extended family are rapidly establishing a new style, the Burnham rug, by adding pictorial figures and densely packed design elements. Audrey Wilson's rug (13) shows the impact Two Grey Hills has had across the reservation at Indian Wells.

8

Bessie Lee

b. 1921

Red Mesa/Teec Nos Pos

Clans: *Bit'ahnii* (within his cover people); born for *Tó dích'íi'nii* (bitter water people)

Bessie Lee has woven other rugs very similar in pattern, coloration, and size to this one. Lee's rugs, in turn, differ only in coloration from a rug woven by Emma Yabeney in 1962 that is now in the collection of the Heard Museum. Photographs of other weavers' rugs, including the 1974 *Arizona Highways* illustration of Yabeney's popular rug, sit on a dresser near one of Lee's looms.

Lee weaves the geometric Teec Nos Pos style in a strict sense, with aniline and natural colors, central panels, and multiple borders. She duplicates the proportions and layout of earlier rugs but varies individual elements slightly to create a new overall unity each time. The X shapes in the inner and outer borders of this rug are leitmotifs of her family's style. The central double rectangles and geometric motifs with hooks or frets are common Teec features. Teec weavers frequently include pictorial filler motifs such as weaving combs and bows and arrows; in this rug, Lee uses stylized feathers.

A soft, natural gray, accented with a strong red and deep brown, typically forms the background of Lee's Teec Nos Pos rugs. Her bold borders usually have black backgrounds. Unlike the many Teec weavers who use green, purple, and orange accents, Lee avoids bright colors. She eschews the four-ply commercial yarns that were the standard for Teec rugs during the 1970s before single-ply processed wool became common, although many who weave in this style still use them. Lee also excels at Red Mesa serrate-outline rugs, which she combines with her characteristic black-background borders.

Just east of Teec Nos Pos, the strip of highway between Shiprock and Farmington is dotted with more than two dozen wholesalers, retailers, and pawnshops that buy and sell rugs. While a few weavers sell exclusively to one buyer, many take bids on their rugs at Jed Foutz's Shiprock Trading Company, Tom Wheeler's Hogback Trading Company, Bob French's Navajo Rugs, and other enterprises along "the strip." Well-known and respected on the strip, Lee sometimes spends an entire day driving from store to store in her pickup, "taking bids" on a rug before sealing a bargain. Her husband, Ray, usually accompanies her and, unlike most Navajo husbands, sometimes helps negotiate the price. By shopping around for the highest bid, Lee gains a wider exposure for her rugs and builds her reputation. She also learns which buyers prefer her rugs and, perhaps most significantly, preserves her independence.

Teec Nos Pos Rug 1983

Provenance: Ray Gwilliam, Phoenix, Arizona, 1983; to Gwilliam's partner, Steve Getzwiller, Benson, Arizona; acquired July 1983

1983.84

Dimensions: 160.5 x 122 cm. (63 x 48 in.)

Tapestry weave, diagonal and interlocked joins

Warp: handspun wool, z, natural white, 11/in.
Weft: processed wool, z, aniline black, red, gray-brown, gray, dark rust red, dark brown, red-brown, natural white, 36/in.; commercial yarn, z, tan-brown, 52/in.
Selvage cords: warp—processed wool, 2z-S, aniline black, 2-strand twining; weft—paired warps, no twining

9

Mamie P. Begay

b. 1949

Sweetwater/Teec Nos Pos

Clans: *Bit'ahnii* (within his cover people), born for *Áshiihí* (salt people)

Mamie Begay comes from the Sweetwater area, about ten miles south of Red Mesa and twenty southeast of Teec Nos Pos. Since she and her late husband, Ernest, left there seventeen years ago, she has lived all over the reservation. In the 1980s, the couple spent several years at Navajo, New Mexico, near the sawmill where Ernest worked. Then, with their young daughter and three sons, they moved to Steamboat and later to Ganado, both in Arizona. Throughout their travels, Begay wove the serrate-outline rugs for which her home community is renowned. Photographs of the Teec Nos Pos Trading Post booth at the 1912 Shiprock Fair show rugs with patterns almost indistinguishable from Begay's (James 1988:33). Begay learned weaving from her grandmother at the age of twelve and began teaching her own six-year-old daughter, Marlena, in 1988.

Begay sells many of her large, finely outlined rugs at the Crownpoint Rug Auction on the eastern edge of the reservation. She tries to have a new one ready every six weeks, in time to consign it to the evening-long sale held in the Crownpoint Elementary School gymnasium. Since Mamie is the only Teec Nos Pos weaver bringing such eye dazzlers to Crownpoint, her rugs usually elicit "oohs" and "aahs" from the audience. A photograph of one of her unmistakable rugs appeared in the Winter 1989 *Native Peoples* magazine, along with an anecdote about the frenzied bidding and applause it received (Hirschmann 1989:8).

The Crownpoint Rug Weavers Association auction is a move toward self-determination for members like Begay. After bringing in their rugs and establishing a minimum price, weavers usually watch the sale from the back of the room with their families. Paid the evening of the sale, each takes home 90% of her rug's final price. Members also receive an annual dividend from association earnings. Auction prices are generally higher than those a wholesale purchaser would pay, but lower than retail, so both weavers and buyers win. Weavers from across the reservation—as far as Pinon, Tuba City, and Shonto—come to the sales. Like Begay, many weave on a regular schedule just to keep up with the auctions.

Bidding is fierce and exciting, and a rug is sold "every thirty seconds," according to one auctioneer. Buyers usually number several hundred on a summer evening and include traders and foreign tourists, local doctors and visiting anthropologists. Rugs range from standard regional styles to pictorials and maverick experiments. With prices from under ten dollars to several thousand, there is something for everyone.

I found Mamie Begay's rug at the auction preview, when all 375 rugs for sale were heaped onto folding tables for the crowd to rummage through. I jotted down its number, got a bidding card, and seated myself in the second row amid an audience of about 400. At seven o'clock, three auctioneers came on stage and began holding up one rug after another as their fast-paced patter blared out over the public address system. Begay's rug came up sometime around ten, and after a quick volley of bidding that almost doubled the starting price, it belonged to the Ross collection. The auction went on until nearly midnight, when weavers and buyers formed lines to settle up.

Teec Nos Pos/Red Mesa Rug 1988

Provenance: Acquired Crownpoint Rug Weavers Association Auction, Crownpoint, New Mexico, July 1988

1988.111

Dimensions: 223.0 x 138.0 cm. (88 x 54½ in.)

Tapestry weave, diagonal and dovetailed joins

Warp: processed wool yarn, z, natural white, 7/in.
Weft: handspun and processed wool yarns, z, natural and aniline dyed colors, 48/in.
Selvage cords: warp—processed wool, 3z-S, aniline or vegetal peach, 2-strand twining; weft—single 3-ply cord as outer warp, no twining

10
Daisy Tauglechee
1909-1990
Two Grey Hills, New Mexico

Daisy Tauglechee's death in 1990 marked the end of a long, distinguished weaving career. Throughout her life, she set unprecedented standards of fine spinning, superbly even textures, subtle coloration, and well-balanced patterns. Largely through her work, the weaving from her home area of Two Grey Hills had gained a superlative reputation by the late 1940s. The Tauglechee name remains synonymous with the best of the style. Tauglechee and her work have appeared in *Arizona Highways* magazine, in books, and on postcards. In 1959, trader Gilbert Maxwell paid a record $1,100 for one of Tauglechee's rugs. He later wrote, "Daisy Togelchee [sic] of Toadlena is without doubt in my estimation the greatest living Navajo weaver. A good Navajo rug may have thirty weft threads to the inch—Mrs. Togelchee will average 100 weft threads, and some of her work has an astounding 115 weft threads to the

inch!" (1963:28). Kathy Foutz of the Russell Foutz Indian Room in Farmington, New Mexico, says Tauglechee was probably "the best spinner that ever lived. I've never seen any one else who could make such thin and even threads. There are a lot of excellent weavers out there, but Daisy was tops."

In the late 1940s, the Denver Art Museum acquired its first Tauglechee rug, a stellar example of the early Two Grey Hills style (fig. 7). Thirty-five years later, when the tapestry now in the Ross collection was woven, Tauglechee was a great-grandmother in her seventies. Differences between the two rugs reflect trends in Navajo weaving in general, in the Two Grey Hills style specifically, and in Tauglechee's own maturation. The Ross rug's smaller size, higher number of threads per inch, and even more regular selvages represent changes noted reservation-wide since the 1940s. In the early Two Grey Hills style, rectangular motifs in a rectangular panel were more common than the central diamond shapes that later prevailed. Tauglechee's own simplicity of design and limited suite of colors, always apparent in her work, became even more pronounced in her later years.

As her eyesight began to fail, Daisy Tauglechee worked closely with her daughter-in-law, Priscilla Tauglechee, a fine weaver in her own right. Their collaboration allowed Daisy to continue creating a few rugs each year, even though she suffered from Parkinson's disease and eventually grew blind. Priscilla's contribution to this tapestry's design can be seen in the elongated central diamond with large, prominent corner triangles, sometimes called "frog's feet." Daisy's virtuosity is particularly evident in the fine spinning and carefully blended colors, features she created in both her own and Priscilla's tapestries as long as she was able.

Two Grey Hills Tapestry 1982
Provenance: Ray Gwilliam, Phoenix, Arizona, spring 1982; to Gwilliam's partner, Steve Getzwiller, Benson, Arizona; acquired May 1982

1982.51

Dimensions: 72.5 x 42.5 cm.
(28½ x 17 in.)

Tapestry weave, interlocked and diagonal joins

Warp: commercial yarn, split and respun, s, shiny white, 18/in.
Weft: handspun wool, z, aniline top-dyed black, natural white, natural brown, natural blended gray, 60-70/in.
Selvage cords: warp—handspun, 2z-S, natural white, 2-strand twining; weft—handspun, 2(2z-s)S, natural charcoal gray, 2-strand twining

11

Barbara Jean Teller Ornelas

b. 1954

Tucson, Arizona

Clans: *Tábaahá* (edge water people), born for *Tó 'aheedlíinii* (water flows together people)

Barbara Ornelas comes from a well-known family of weavers that includes her mother, Ruth Teller, and her grandmother, Susie Tom. Ornelas weaves thinly spun, naturally colored wools into perfectly symmetrical compositions that reflect the influence of Daisy Tauglechee and the ensuing generation of Two Grey Hills weavers. By selling at Santa Fe Indian Market and directly to clients, demonstrating at museums and galleries, and openly voicing her views of the craft, Ornelas has, however, taken a more public role than any of her neighbors or relatives.

After four years of work, Barbara and her sister, Rosann Teller Lee, completed a large Two Grey Hills tapestry that won Best of Show at the 1987 Santa Fe Indian Market. This was an exceptional accomplishment for a number of reasons. Under any circumstances,

four years is a long time to maintain consistency in weaving. But midway through production, Ornelas and her husband David moved to Phoenix so he could attend college, and she was forced to make a long commute to her parents' reservation home to work on the rug. Disagreements often prompted one or the other sister to threaten to quit the project.

A Navajo rug had never before taken the Best of Show ribbon at the Santa Fe Indian Market, but this tapestry was technically and aesthetically extraordinary. It was made entirely from handcarded and handspun yarn. The natural wool was fine and even, the weaving consistent and controlled, the colors delicately graded and harmonious, and the design balanced and beautifully varied. Measuring a whopping 5 by 8½ feet with 95 to 108 wefts per inch, it set a new record for contemporary Navajo rug prices when it sold for $60,000 to a Texas investor. The sisters paid their backlog of bills and returned to their respective looms in Arizona and New Mexico. Part of Ornelas's earnings paid for David's graduate training in pharmacology at the University of Arizona.

Though she finished her first rug when she was eight, Ornelas was "kind of embarrassed to weave. I was embarrassed that my mom was a weaver, hanging on to the old ways." After high school, she completed a year of business college in Phoenix, then worked as a secretary. In 1980 she married David, who was then working in a bank. Their daughter, Sierra, was born in 1981, and a son, Michael, in 1985. "Through my husband's eyes, I saw weaving in a different light, as something special that should be carried on. At home, you see someone weaving every day, but to him, it was special."

Ornelas remembers how difficult it was to learn from her mother: "Her

way of weaving was to do it the way you feel, but I didn't know how to feel at the time. I didn't know how to listen to myself, but she expected me to." Ornelas took a different tack with Sierra by turning learning into a game.

Major influences on Ornelas's work include her mother, grandmothers, and older sister. "My mom used to set up my loom for me, do all my wool. I'd weave two-thirds of it, then she'd finish it for me. Then I'd call it all my own! When we lived in Phoenix, if I made a mistake, I'd get on the phone to Two Grey Hills. My sister Rosann taught me a lot about the finesse of weaving. To get help, I used to take my loom home on the Greyhound bus—can you believe it?" Nowadays her technical problems are largely solved through her own cumulative experience, but sharing goes on. Sketches for patterns pass back and forth between Ruth, Rosann, and Ornelas. "I think of it as a compliment when someone borrows my patterns." Though she has expanded her repertoire to include variations on the Burntwater style, Ornelas still creates intricate Two Grey Hills patterns, now in shades of pale pink, blue, purple, yellow, gray, and white. Although smaller than the prize-winning 1987 tapestry, Ornelas's Ross collection rug is equally refined and shows the skill and artistry of a thoroughly dedicated weaver.

Ornelas and her husband systematically market her work by getting recognition, finding competitions, and setting prices. She carries business cards that read, "Barbara Jean Teller Ornelas, Master Navajo Weaver, Specializing in Two Grey Hills, Burntwater, Ganado, Miniatures, Demonstrations." Ornelas is one of only a handful of weavers who take rugs to the annual Santa Fe Indian Market. Few can afford to stockpile their rugs for the show. In 1991, she once again took

Best of Show in Santa Fe, and a small Burntwater piece won the 1991 Award for Excellence in Navajo Weaving sponsored by Gloria Ross.

But Ornelas's goal is not just to win prizes and promote herself. As a member of the "Traditional Ethnic Visual Arts" selection panel for the Arizona Commission on the Arts, Ornelas encourages ethnic artists around the state to get involved in commission-sponsored school and community programs. Her goals reflect her experiences as a weaver: "I'd like to see Navajo weaving [considered] an art, not just a craft. I grew up watching my grandparents work so hard and get nothing. I feel like weaving has already given me what I've needed—money and recognition—and I'd like to see it continue to make a living for other people, too."

Two Grey Hills Tapestry 1989

Provenance: Acquired Indian Market, Santa Fe, New Mexico, August 1989

1989.119

Dimensions: 93.0 x 60.0 cm. (36½ x 24 in.)

Tapestry weave, interlocked joins

Warp: handspun wool, z, natural white, 13/in.
Weft: handspun wool, z, aniline top-dyed black, natural blended gray, natural white, natural dark brown, natural blended light brown, 80/in.
Selvage cords: warp—handspun wool, 2z-Z, natural blended light gray, 2-strand twining; weft—handspun wool, 2z-Z, natural blended light gray, 3-strand twining

12

Bessie Barber

b. 1955

Aneth, Utah

Clans: *Naakaii dine'é* (Mexican people); born for *Hooghan lání* (many hogans people)

Bessie Barber and one of her sisters joke about how, since Bessie's move to Utah, they keep in touch only through rug-selling trips to their dealer in Durango, Colorado. But these trips are a relatively new development in the family's history. After finishing high school in the early 1970s, Barber learned to weave from her mother, Anna Mae Barber, who also taught her three youngest daughters and the three young sisters she adopted after her mother died. For years, the women in this extended family all lived in Burnham, New Mexico, and sold their rugs for as little as $75 every six weeks at the Crownpoint Rug Weavers Association auctions. Although they were finely textured,

handcarded, and handspun in lovely natural colors, these rugs were fairly modest works. The women made the sixty-five mile trip because the prices they received were fair and being able to set a minimum price gave them some control over the sale.

The Burnham style didn't begin in earnest until 1980, when several of the young women in the Barber/ Begay family decided to develop a distinctive style by diverging from the local Two Grey Hills tradition in significant ways. They used only native, handspun sheep wool but added small accents of bright dyes. Their complex designs were sometimes asymmetrical and pictorial, in contrast to the strict geometric symmetry of Two Grey Hills. To gain more economic control over their weaving, they sought a new buyer for their unusual rugs and found Jackson Clark II of Toh Atin Gallery in Durango, Colorado. A third-generation native arts dealer, Clark had shifted the business away from trading for Indian rugs and baskets to the gallery-style promotion of individual Native American artists. In the large Burnham rugs, he saw the potential for sales in the thousands of dollars.

Burnham style rugs and tapestries take time to produce. "The whole family works together," Barber says. Her five brothers shear the sheep and make the looms, battens, and forks. The women spend long hours working the wool—cleaning, picking, teasing, carding, spinning, and respinning. Often, an older woman in the family makes the yarn. All of the women stress quality standards: "Sometimes you have to take all your time to come out with a real good rug, so it just takes all your patience." Much of the wool comes from family flocks, but Jackson Clark provides some from the Utah State University *churro* flock. The finest and strongest warp is a

handspun combination of sheep wool and Angora-goat mohair.

Burnham weavers achieve a highly energized style by compressing design elements into shallow, horizontal shapes and packing them densely together. The very fine threads they use help make this compression possible. In Bessie Barber's rug, it can be seen in the inner and outer border motifs and the flattened, stylized plant forms that divide the three middle panels. Although some Burnham designs look accordian-pleated, the effect is less pronounced here because the middle panels have balanced proportions.

Small *yé'ii bicheii* dancers, baskets, and other ceremonial motifs in otherwise geometric patterns make many Burnham rugs easy to recognize. The weavers share design ideas through a notebook of sketches. They also get ideas from magazines, books, and rugs they see in trading posts or at auctions.

As Jackson Clark points out, "When this started, the young girls all lived together at Burnham in a family compound." In the eight years since then, the core group has scattered, spreading the style to other communities. Clark thinks it may be the first time a group of weavers has initiated a new style "without the influence of traders, chapter houses, or someone else."

As buyer, Clark gives advice on the overall technical quality of the rugs, but stays out of the designing. One of the sisters notes, "The designs— we take care of that. We think about our designs, and Jackson actually just tells us to take our time on it so the rug can be real good. . . . He'll know when we're in a rush, and he'll tell us to slow down."

None of the women claims to be a strict adherent to traditional Navajo religion, despite the religious emblems in their rugs. One says, "I don't really follow the Navajo religion. I still believe in it, but I usually don't really get myself into it." Several are Christians who attend church regularly and have crucifixes and rosaries in their homes. Family members differ in their knowledge of taboos against using Navajo religious imagery in their rugs, but all agree that such beliefs no longer apply. A grandfather once told one of the sisters that natural sheep wool should never go into a *yé'ii* or *yé'ii bicheii* rug. This prohibition clearly carries no weight in the Barber/ Begay family, but it may explain why *yé'ii* rug weavers from Shiprock once used only commercial yarns.

Ten years ago there were only three weavers in this family; five years ago there were nine; and in 1991 there were fourteen. The core weavers of the new Burnham style include Anna Mae Barber, her sisters (Alice, Helen, and Sandy Begay), her daughters (Laverne, Lorene, and Bessie), and her nieces (seventeen-year-old Teresa and nine-year-old Julia). Even the sister of a brother-in-law now uses the Burnham style.

Burnham Rug 1988

Provenance: Toh Atin Gallery, Durango, Colorado; acquired October 1988

1988.167

Dimensions: 133.5 x 94.0 cm. (52½ x 37 in.)

Tapestry weave, interlocked and diagonal joins

Warp: handspun wool, z, natural white, 12/in.
Weft: handspun wool, z, natural, vegetal and aniline colors, 50-60/in.
Selvage cords: handspun wool, 2z-S, natural white, 2-strand twining

13

Audrey Spencer Wilson

b. 1920

Indian Wells, Arizona

Clans: *Tó dích'íi'nii* (bitter water people); born for *Ma'ii deeshgiizhnii* (coyote pass people)

T hough it was made hundreds of miles from Two Grey Hills, Audrey Wilson's rug was clearly inspired by that region's style. It may be called "Two Grey Hills" because of its gray, brown, black, and white colors and fancy central diamond with reciprocating border. Traditional Two Grey Hills rugs contain a natural brown wool, sometimes carded with white to create lighter shades. But this rug gets its light brown color from white wool that has soaked in a dilute bath of walnut-hull dye.

Wilson began the rug in February 1980; in August it was nearly half completed, and by January 1981 it was finished. At one point, she made one of the black motifs too large and had to reweave the entire area. While the rug was on the loom, Wilson also

made baskets, sash belts, god's-eye medallions, and doilies in a local arts and crafts program.

Wilson usually uses complex two-faced and fancy weaves and designs that incorporate *yé'ii* figures (29). Perhaps because her job taxed her time and energy, she chose the simpler tapestry-weave technique for this rug. "I decided to change my loom for weaving this one because I wanted to see how I would do it," Wilson says. "When I was a little girl, this was the first kind I learned. I started to use it again, even though I've got my two-faced kind now. This is just a regular, old-fashioned way of weaving."

Wilson has always taken pleasure in large, ambitious projects. A self-taught weaver, she feels she gets a higher rate of return for one high-quality, time-consuming rug than she would for several smaller, rapidly woven rugs. Rather than using expedient lazy lines, she prefers to pass her yarn across the full width of a design area to create an unmarred surface. Her attention to detail pays off in the prices she commands. Even though she'd never made a Two Grey Hills rug before, she was drawn by the inherent challenge and the style's market appeal.

A small, tarpaper-covered shed houses Wilson's weaving operation—a large, adjustable, lumber loom, abundant bags of raw sheep fleece and yarn, and, hanging from the rafters, dried plants and barks for dyes. She and her elderly brother use a commercial, Penguin-brand spinning wheel to tighten the twist on 4-ply commercial knitting worsted used on sash belts.

Asked what she thinks about when she's weaving, the pragmatic Wilson responds in heavily accented English, "I think about weaving the design; that is what I usually do. I just think about it—how I'm going to do it, what it will look like, how I'm going to put it up." She never sketches her

designs before weaving: "I just had it in my mind, like I always say. I just used my mind with these patterns." And once the rug is off the loom? "I think about where I'm going to sell it, and who is going to buy it. I don't think about the next rug until I get the yarn for it."

Two Grey Hills Rug 1981

Provenance: Acquired January 1981

1983.118

Dimensions: 179.0 x 122.0 cm. (70 x 47½ in.)

Tapestry weave, interlocked and stepped diagonal joins

Warp: handspun wool, z, natural white, 11/in.
Weft: handspun wool, z, aniline top-dyed black, natural white, natural gray, walnut-hull dyed brown, 40/in.
Selvage cords: handspun wool, 2z-S, aniline top-dyed black, 2-strand twining

Color has symbolic meaning to Navajos when used in specific religious contexts. In sandpainting, for instance, the cardinal directions, gender, precious ceremonial materials, and meteorological phenomena all have complex relationships with certain colors and color combinations (Reichard 1950:187-207, 214-216). In weaving, though, color seems to have no importance beyond its aesthetic impact. One weaver explains her choice of colors: "Red is my favorite color with white. It shows more. I usually make my rugs with red and gray and white. The colors stand out and are pretty." "I guess people have different tastes in colors," another experienced weaver muses. "A lot of people like red; a lot of people like purple and pink. I have my own colors: orange and green and brown."

"In the olden days, they didn't use very many colors. They used their own wool—sheared their own sheep and spun their own everything. The white was natural and the gray was natural. But since we started using those vegetable dyes, we use all different kinds of bushes and herbs and roots that make different colors. Now we have colorful rugs!"

As Philomena Yazzie notes, Navajo weavers used native plant dyes sparingly, if at all, before the twentieth century. Their colors more often came from the natural tones of sheep wool and from imported dyes like indigo blue, cochineal and lac reds (in the form of raveled fabrics), and synthetic dyes known as "anilines." By the late nineteenth century, they had added a colorful array of commercial yarns to this limited palette. But rugs containing mostly natural white, grays, and black and aniline red still outnumbered eye dazzlers made with aniline-dyed Germantown yarns. Weavers didn't start using vegetal colors extensively until the early part of this century (fig. 8).

Many Ross collection rugs show how deeply vegetal dyes have taken root in the Navajo weaving tradition, especially in the Wide Ruins, Pine Springs, Chinle, Crystal, and Burntwater styles. Each style has its own distinct origins, aesthetics, patrons, and practitioners, but they all express the abundant creativity of weavers experimenting with the variety of colors available from plants.

Explorations of vegetal-colored rug styles follow many paths. Marjorie Spencer (14), Irene Clark (15, 16) and Ella Rose Perry (17) all returned to weaving late in life, after their families were established; each has personalized the regional style in which she works. Spencer weaves meticulous Wide Ruins rugs that subtly combine many more colors than are usually found in that style. Clark adds to the Crystal style her own strong, closely modulated earth tones to create trend-setting rugs. Perry adopted the local style when she moved to Crystal for a job, and now no one can match her combinations of pale and stark colors and her smooth textures. Lifelong weaver Philomena Yazzie (18) helped establish the Burntwater style by combining a startling array of colors with new bordered designs. Today she is imitated widely, but her work still stands apart visually and technically. In adopting the Burntwater style, Jennie Thomas (19) breaks with the Wide Ruins style to respond to market trends and her own penchant for pastels. In the remote community of Three Turkey Ruins, Helen Bia (20) practices a localized style with green and yellow tones used only by her immediate family. Kalley Musial (21) makes expressive rugs whose smoky, complex color schemes have no regional affiliation but, rather, derive from her own feelings and her life's daily events. Following in her mother's footsteps, Kalley's daughter, Jenny (22), explores color and texture according to her moods.

Dyeing with native plants requires special knowledge—which plants to use, when and where to find them, how to harvest certain plant parts, how to extract colors, and how to fix

8. Wide Ruins rug, 1940s. Denver Art Museum: Gift of Frederic H. Douglas. 1954.388

the dye into yarn. "Dyeing wool is a lot of work," one expert comments. "You have to go out there and get all kinds of plants. Then you come home and boil the water over an open fire. It needs a lot of work." Since it is so difficult to duplicate a color, dyers generally try to make enough dye for an entire rug. Although families and clans share recipes and some are widely known and even published, every dyer's method is slightly different, and individuals are often known for the inimitable colors in their rugs.

The identification of a color's source is not always easy. Weavers use the all-purpose term "vegetable" to refer to plant dyes they extract from leaves, stems, bark, and roots. Most know only the common Navajo names for the plants they use. To complicate things further, weavers may add synthetic dyes, KoolAid, battery acid, rusty nails, horseshoes, crepe paper, or instant coffee to the dye bath. Because only the weaver knows which dyestuffs are used to make any given color, I've used vegetal-*colored* here to describe colors that resemble those from plants (but that could have come from any number of sources), as opposed to vegetal-*dyed*, those that definitely come only from plants.

Many weavers who make their own plant dyes also use commercial vegetal-colored yarns. In an innovative project begun in the late 1970s, traders Steve Getzwiller and Bruce Burnham paid expert Navajo dyers to home-dye white and gray yarns they provided. At first, the traders gave these dyed yarns only to commissioned weavers. But now, weavers from all over the country can choose from as many as 250 of these home-dyed colors at Burnham's trading post in Sanders. The dyers do not document their

ingredients, and any one color may include a variety of native and imported dyestuffs. For would-be dyers, using these pre-colored yarns might discourage experimentation and creativity, but they can give beginners a boost that makes the difference between continuing or not. And in the hands of a skillful weaver, these yarns can greatly enhance a rug's visual appeal.

14

Marjorie Spencer

b. 1936

Wide Ruins, Arizona

Clans: *Kiyaa'áanii* (towering house people); born for *Dibé lizhiní* (black sheep people)

The Wide Ruins regional style originated in the late 1930s and early 1940s. Encouraged by area traders Sally and Bill Lippincott, weavers developed new plant dyes, elaborated on 100-year-old borderless, striped patterns, and quickly established an attractive style all their own.

Some writers distinguish the Wide Ruins style from the neighboring Pine Springs style, but there are few, if any, actual differences. Both areas use geometric, serrated, often finely outlined motifs arranged in zoned bands that alternate with plain and "beaded" bands. The same vegetal-dyed palette characterizes both. The similarity shouldn't be surprising, since weavers from both areas sell to the same traders, and many maintain homes in both areas or have moved from one to the other.

During the 1960s and 1970s, Wide Ruins and Pine Springs weavers were known for vegetal-dyed, earthtone golds, yellows, and browns accented with natural sheep-wool grays and white. But in the 1980s, when Burnham's trading post at Sanders introduced many new home-dyed yarns, weavers began to use chic shades of mauve, lavendar, purple, pink, salmon, and blue. Traders suggested that earthtones no longer sold well and advised weavers to concentrate on the decorator colors of the eighties. Says Spencer, "I used to like brown and gold, but now buyers are not interested in those colors. At first I didn't care for the pinks and blues, but I'm getting interested now."

She and her four daughters have made good use of the variety of new vegetal-colored yarns. With the range of colors now available, Spencer says, "I do more design, more work, and more thinking about what goes together." In her Ross collection rug she has included sixteen different colors. A saleswoman at the Sanders store reports that one of Spencer's daughters may drop in several times in the same week to find new yarns for a rug in progress.

Marjorie Spencer learned to weave when she was 27, after her own family was established, but this has not slowed her progress or compromised her quality. Today she is known as one of the best Wide Ruins weavers. Like Irene Clark of Crystal, she was strongly influenced by Hubbell trader Bill Young, who encouraged and critiqued her weaving.

Spencer's daughters are all becoming well-known and respected weavers. Like their mother, several didn't learn until adulthood, after they finished high school or some college. Raised predominantly in Mormon foster homes after their father left the family, they have only recently come back to the reservation to weave with their mother. They say that going to school away from the reservation has given them the perspective to appreciate the Navajo weaving tradition and that classes in art and literature stimulated them to explore their own talents.

Spencer inspires her daughters to experiment with color and design while maintaining strict standards of technique. They all agree that she encourages their weaving without pushing them into it. Spencer and three of her daughters—Vera Spencer, Irma Spencer Owens, and Geneva Scott Shabie—usually make rugs in the Wide Ruins style; Brenda Spencer often weaves Burntwater patterns. Brenda works at Hubbell Trading Post and was featured in *A Separate Vision*, a recent Museum of Northern Arizona exhibition with companion videotape and publications (Eaton 1989, 1990). Selected for the project because of her role as an independent, recognized artist, she represents a growing trend among young native people.

The Spencer women all rely on the income from their weaving. One daughter acknowledges, "I think I make more out of weaving than working [outside the home]. Comparing the price of a rug and the wage you get at a job, I get more making a rug." But money doesn't drive them to weave: "Some ladies aren't working and don't weave. We wonder what they do besides cook and clean! When we finish our rugs and don't have anything to do, we just want something to start up again. I think it's our habit." Irma Spencer Owens emphasizes weaving's creative potential: "I see it as an art—something I create on my own."

Wide Ruins Rug 1988

Provenance: Hubbell Trading Post, Ganado, Arizona, 1988; acquired July 1988

1988.88

Dimensions: 151.0 x 107.0 cm. (59½ x 42 in.)

Tapestry weave, interlocked joins

Warp: handspun or respun processed wool, z, natural white, 12/in.
Weft: processed wool yarn, z, natural and vegetal colors, 48-60/in.
Selvage cords: processed wool yarn, handplied, 3z-S, dyed tan on natural gray, 3-strand twining

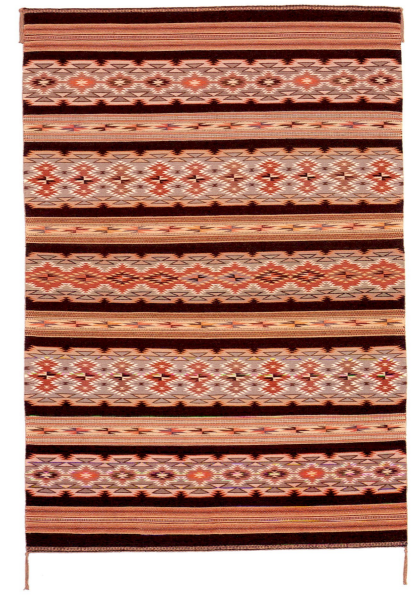

15

Irene Clark

b. 1934

Crystal, New Mexico

Clans: *Tábaahá* (water's edge people); born for *Honágháahnii* (he walks around one people)

Earlier this century, weavers in the Chuska Mountain community of Crystal made bordered, boldly geometric rugs inspired partly by Oriental carpets. These "Early Crystal" rugs, as they are now known, followed suggestions made by local trader J. B. Moore and used a palette of natural gray, black, and white with touches of red. Sometime during the 1940s, a modern Crystal style developed based on zoned bands and marked by nubby, handcarded and handspun wool in strong, vegetal-dyed colors.

In the sixties, Irene Clark and her mother, well-known weaver Glenabah Hardy, began to evolve a distinctive, richly colored version of the Crystal style. Clark now guides her daughter Teresa Clark, daughters-in-law Evelyna and Julie, and sister-in-law Marjorie Hardy. As one of the younger women says, "It's fun. It keeps your mind busy. If you have nothing to do, you can weave." Clark also once taught at the Crystal chapter house, where, she

notes diplomatically, "Some young ladies learned better than others."

Irene Clark works with very smoothly carded, handspun or processed yarns. Controlled weaving, straight sides, and beautiful 3-strand twined edging are all trademarks of her style; most weavers use 2-strand twining. Her color sense is a more subtle version of the bold, hot, almost acid, vegetal-dyed colors of the Crystal tradition. Clark says she chooses her colors "according to Mother Nature. Like the greens—I see that vegetation is green. The dirt is brown. Orange and yellow—it seems like they represent the flower and rainbow colors." She adds, "Well, I guess it's just how you dress sometimes. If you're going to have red shoes, you need something that will match, like a light gray shirt or pants, or anything that will match. That's how I put my colors in my rugs."

Crystal rugs are sometimes confused with those from Wide Ruins and Chinle. Crystals tend to be bolder in color and pattern than Wide Ruins, and somewhat more complex in both color combinations and patterning than Chinle, the simplest of all vegetal styles. In general, Crystal rugs contain darker earth tones; Wide Ruins and Chinle styles tend more to pastels. Two features that set apart modern Crystal rugs most are their so-called "wavy lines" and "termination panels." A weaver creates wavy lines by repeatedly alternating two colors of weft across the width of a rug, so that a wiggly pinstripe effect results. While Wide Ruins rugs may have several passes of wavy lines only at the edges of solid colored areas, Crystal weaving usually uses them throughout the entire rug. "Termination panels"— wider solid or wavy-line bands— appear at each end of a Crystal rug. Wide Ruins rugs rarely have termination panels; their designs appear ready to extend beyond the rug's edges.

Irene Clark has lived in Crystal nearly all her life. She speaks both English and Navajo and generally dresses in slacks and tailored blouses or jeans and T-shirts. Her parents kept her at home to herd sheep until she was about twelve, when she attended five years of school, where she met her husband, Jimmy. They had seven children, five of whom survive; three have attended college and one recently graduated from high school. Surrounded by a flower garden and picket fence, Clark's large frame home is decorated with family photographs and certificates of appreciation awarded to her husband during his career with the tribal government's Water Resources Division.

Clark started weaving in earnest only about fifteen years ago, after most of her children were grown. Her skills and reputation rose quickly, and encouragement came mainly from the late Bill Young, a trader at the Hubbell post. "Every time I took a rug down there, [Young] would tell me, 'Looky here, Irene, this is where the mistake is,'" she recalls. "And then he'd say, 'Don't ever get mad when I tell you that. Some ladies get mad and don't like to be told about their mistakes.' He told me how to match my colors and gave me other ideas. He once told me, 'Someday, Irene, you'll be a good weaver, maybe even the best.' My mom was a weaver and used to make big rugs. So even though she taught me, I now teach her back how to match her colors. When [Young] retired, I made him a little rug."

Clark is a prolific weaver, yet she runs a large and active household: "Most of the time, I stay home in order to maintain a healthy household. The day begins with cooking for the family, cleaning the house, feeding the livestock, and then I finally weave from around 8:30 until noon. At that time I'll take lunch, check the livestock, and go back to weaving until four. By then, the family will be coming home, so

I'll start supper, feed the livestock, and start weaving again until bedtime. It's a full-time workday."

A conscientious weaver, Clark intentionally sets an example for the younger women in her family. She tells them, "the more you weave, the more easily designs will come to you." She has a carefully articulated, matter-of-fact approach to her work: "This rug I'm making, somebody's going to like it and somebody won't like it. It's always like that. There's all kinds of people. You want more money, so you put more design in it. You have to really watch your edges and your design, where you might make a mistake." Maria Saltclaw, a sister who doesn't weave, comments, "Weaving takes your whole head. You need to know science and math, especially algebra and geometry. Irene's designs are outrageous. Our mother says that she outdesigns even her. Some of these weavers, like my sister, are real professionals."

Crystal Rug 1983

Provenance: Steve Getzwiller, Benson, Arizona, July 1983; acquired July 1983

1983.62

Dimensions: 148.0 x 90.0 cm.
(58 x 35½ in.)

Tapestry weave, diagonal and interlocked joins

Warp: handspun processed wool, z, natural white, 11-12/in.
Weft: handspun processed wool, z, natural white, vegetal orange, gold, light olive green, and dark burnt orange, 40/in.
Selvage cords: handspun wool, 2z-S, natural blended gray, 3-strand twining; braided corner tassels

16

Irene Clark

b. 1934

Crystal, New Mexico

Clans: *Tábaahá* (water's edge people); born for *Honágháahnii* (he walks around one people)

T his rug won Best of Textiles and Best of Show at the 1990 Museum of Northern Arizona Navajo Show. It posed a problem for the judges since it didn't fit into any of the standard categories and yet was clearly a superior technical and visual accomplishment. Although Clark is from Crystal and the rug includes some typical Crystal "wavy line" weaving at each end, its unusual color scheme and solid gray border excluded it from the Crystal category (15). The judges finally placed it in the "General Rug" category, and it surpassed not only every other rug in the competition, but also the best pieces in every other major category, including jewelry, pottery, basketry, sculpture, and painting.

Clark says the rug represents a new direction she took after several traders told her that Crystal's old-style colors—orange, gold, yellow, green, and brown—were no longer selling. Instead of turning to the pinks, blues, and purples that many weavers are now trying, Clark used terra cotta, khaki, and gray. Although she still most often uses her own vegetal-dyed yarns, she wove this rug with pre-dyed, processed wool yarn.

The similarity between some of this rug's patterns and those on the commercial Pendleton blankets that are popular among Navajos is coincidental, Clark says, although she sees some resemblance in retrospect. She worked out the designs in her mind by rhythmically repeating and varying geometric motifs until they came together in an interesting pattern. None of the motifs has symbolic significance, she says.

She comments on her recent prizes and success with a modest shrug, "I'm proud. I guess I'm up there with the best weavers." It especially pleases her that her family takes an interest. "My husband says, 'I like the design you made last time. It's really pretty. You should make that one again.' Your kids tell you, 'Mom, that looks real pretty. What kind of design are you going to put in? How are you going to make it? How is it going to come out?'"

Though she enjoys her work, Clark takes it very seriously: "Weaving's got some songs, good songs, in it. You don't mess around with a rug. I'm not supposed to tell you [anything except that] it's very sacred. My mom has a song about a rug, but I don't know it. . . . My mom's getting old, and I should learn . . . how to sing it and sing it while I weave. When you finish your rug, you always say a prayer. That will help you again. I do that."

Rug 1990

Provenance: Museum of Northern Arizona gift shop, Flagstaff, Arizona, June 1990; acquired July 1990

Awards: Best of Show, *41st Annual Navajo Artists' Exhibition*, Museum of Northern Arizona, July 1990

1990.187

Dimensions: 162.0 x 119.0 cm. (64 x 47 in.)

Tapestry weave, diagonal and interlocked joins

Warp: processed wool, z, natural white, 9/in.
Weft: processed wool yarn, z, natural, vegetal, and aniline colors, 40/in.
Selvage cords: processed wool yarn, 2z-S, gray, 3-strand twining; braided corner tassels

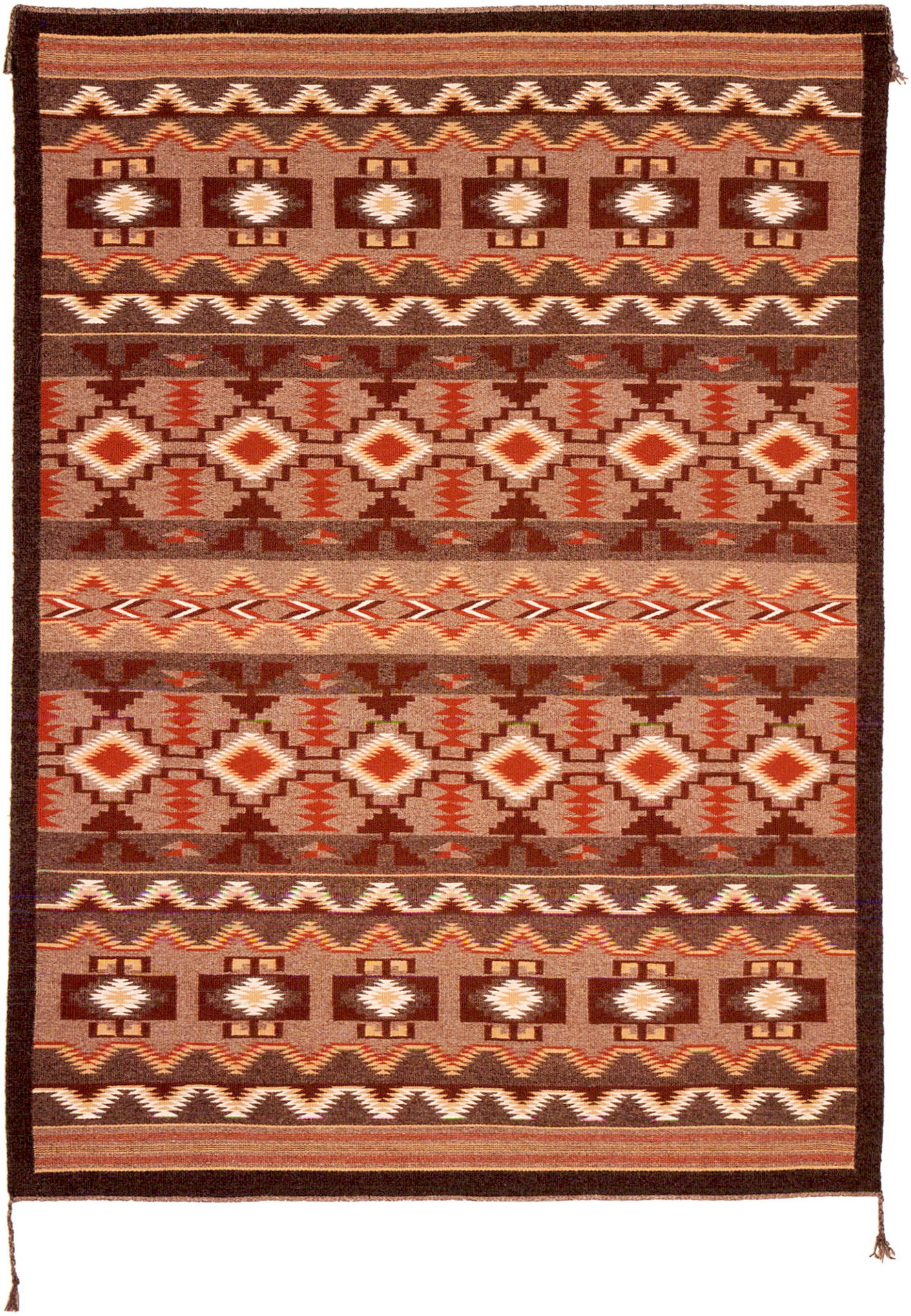

17

Ella Rose Perry

b. 1929

Crystal, New Mexico/St. Michaels, Arizona

Clans: *Naakaii dine'é* (Mexican people); born for *Honágháahnii* (he walks around one people)

Ella Rose Perry's easily recognized version of the Crystal style (15) features soft colors, a smooth but hairy texture like that of fine mohair, and blocky, well-balanced motifs along the "wavy line" bands. Her nearly always perfect side selvages give her rugs an unusual, relaxed flatness. Because of her finesse and personal style, Perry is one of the most respected weavers on the reservation.

Perry was born in St. Michaels, Arizona, just outside Window Rock. Before her recent retirement, she spent thirty years working at the Bureau of Indian Affairs boarding school in Crystal, New Mexico, and she, her husband, and their daughter and three sons lived in school housing. In 1990, with the children grown, she and "Mr. Perry," as she

fondly calls him, moved back to St. Michaels, fifty miles south of Crystal, to be closer to her family.

"Weaving was something given to me by my mom," Perry says. "In my young days, when I was about eight or nine, my mom taught me. My dad always said that I was the one that really did a good job weaving: 'I think you really take after your mom in her work.'

"My mother used to say, 'This is very important for you when you grow up.' She said, 'If a woman knows how to weave, there will be no hunger; you won't get poor; you will always have plenty to eat, plenty of clothes, a good home.' Well, *bilagáana* do their work, get their education; they finish and go on to college and get a good job. My mom said, 'It's different for us. Someday, yes, you will go to school. But someday you will always have this [weaving] and you will remember your great-great-grandmother. That's where it came from, down from the generations. And then from there on, you will teach your grandchildren. Whenever you get married, if your man is lazy and he doesn't work for you, there is your money right there. And there will be plenty to eat, something for you, if you do a good job on this one. You get a good price, you get good money.' She was right, she was right!

"My parents would tease us when we were growing up, too. My dad would say, 'If you know all these things—weaving, cooking, taking care of the hogan, herding and shearing the sheep—then, when you get married, you mother-in-law might be pleased. Because of your weaving, you might be worth twelve horses and she might pay us that many for you!'"

Perry did not weave as a schoolgirl or young mother. She returned to weaving only after she had been employed for several years. Since

then, she has always made Crystal style rugs, with banded patterns in vegetal-dyed colors. She says modestly, "When I was at Crystal, I got kind of interested in what they were doing on that side. So I started [making this style] and I like it. Now I'm known by this style."

Perry is teaching her grown daughter, Marlene, to weave, but the process is a challenge, as it is for many weaving instructors and their pupils. Several times, Ella Rose has set up a loom, and Marlene has begun weaving; weeks later, when Marlene has not returned to the loom, Ella Rose finishes the rug. "I tell her, 'Don't stop; you go on.' Once you stop, once you get away, you get lazy. You have to keep going, keep doing your work. I think that's important."

Perry travels extensively, demonstrating her craft in museums and galleries. She was featured in a recent Land's End mail-order catalog. With rugs in homes from California to New York, Perry takes pride in her network of friends across the country and eagerly welcomes their visits. "It's real nice for me. I get to demonstrate for a lot of *bilagáana*. In my younger days I never dreamed about what I was going to see now. I'm happy that I've met a lot of white people who want rugs."

Crystal Rug 1985

Provenance: Toh Atin Gallery, Durango, Colorado; acquired November 1985

1985.356

Dimensions: 240.0 x 158.0 cm. (95 x 62 in.)

Tapestry weave, interlocked joins

Warp: handspun wool, z, natural white, 11/in.
Weft: handspun wool, z, natural and vegetal colors, 50/in.
Selvage cords: warp—handspun wool, 3z-S, light blended gray, 2-strand twining; weft—handspun wool, 2z-S, light blended gray, 3-strand twining

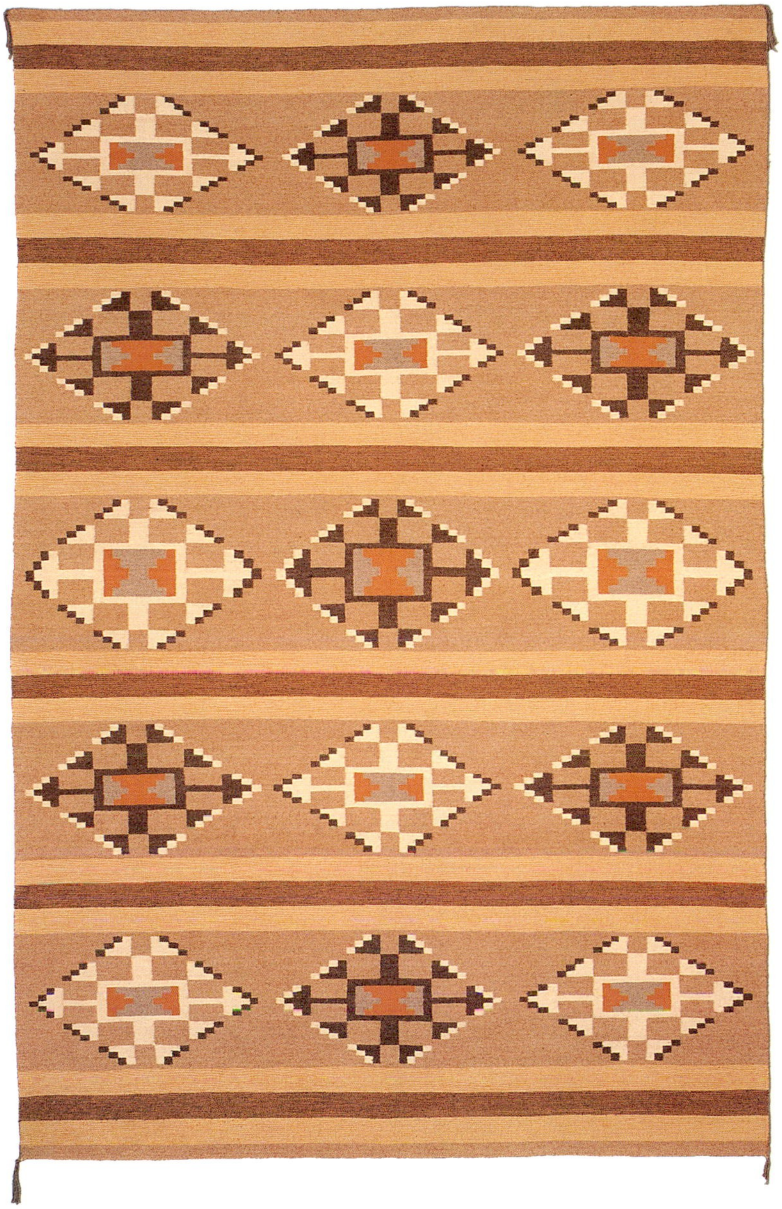

18

Philomena Yazzie

b. 1927

Querino, Arizona

Clans: *Tó dích'íi'nii* (bitter water people); born for *Honágháahnii* (he walks around one people)

Philomena Yazzie is recognized as one of the premier Burntwater weavers, as are her aunt Mary Goldtooth Smith and cousin Maggie Price. Until the late 1960s, the mountain community of Burntwater was not known for any particular weaving style. In 1968, Yazzie made one of the first rugs woven in the style now called "Burntwater," a combination of the bordered central diamond patterns of Ganado and Two Grey Hills and the vegetal-dyed yarns of nearby Wide Ruins and Pine Springs. The use of as many as a dozen colors in one rug, including an unusual blue, characterized her early work, which earned Yazzie first prizes in the New Mexico and Arizona state fairs in 1971 and 1972. When three of her rugs and two by Maggie Price were reproduced in the July 1974 *Arizona Highways*, the Burntwater style was catapulted into the public eye.

The style continued to be woven mainly around Burntwater until the early 1980s, when outside traders

began to sponsor it. Weavers all over the reservation quickly learned that traders wanted Burntwater rugs. On store shelves, skeins of light pink, purple, blue, and other pastel yarns joined the familiar red, gray, black, and white ones. Pastel rugs with central diamonds and fancy borders proliferated. Ironically, for all the impact Yazzie's Burntwater designs had on other weavers, her own daughters do not weave.

Even though she considers weaving a gift not to be abused or overdone, Yazzie is prolific. Throughout the 1980s, she almost always had a large, elaborately patterned Burntwater rug and several smaller ones in progress on her looms. "She weaves all the time," a neighbor notes. Despite her busy schedule, she continued dyeing wool herself with her own combinations of local plants and other materials.

Her work has been imitated and copied both on and off the reservation. A Texas company once reproduced in Belgian-made pile a design that had appeared in *Arizona Highways*. Outraged, Yazzie lacked means to protest. In part because of such violations, she is suspicious of all outsiders and refuses to have her picture taken.

Yazzie is quick to tell you when she has no time to sit around and talk. "I sure don't have time right now. I'm real busy. I have so much to do." In the summer, she rises at 4:30 to herd sheep for several hours before returning to the house to fix meals, babysit her grandchildren, and weave. Her schedule is punctuated by trips to Wyoming to see her children and grandchildren and attend workshops related to her winter job at a school cafeteria. In the past, she has worked as a short-order cook.

Yazzie is now forced by failing eyesight and nagging arthritis to simplify her rug designs and use bolder colors. Her aesthetic sense and

technical control, however, remain superb. One of the first weavers to accept a major commission directly from a museum, she still maintains a waiting list of clients. She also keeps several rugs in progress at once but looks forward to retiring soon and collecting social security. "I'm getting old, and it's just getting too much for me. Besides, I don't have anyone to help. I have to do all the housecleaning, sheepherding, and shopping. It takes almost all day to go to town. So, maybe I'll retire so I can have time on my own." Laughing, she adds, "To sleep and eat and get fat! To take it easy!"

Although she could support herself entirely from weaving, she prefers to juggle her cafeteria job with ambitious weaving projects. Together they provide financial security for the long term: weaving brings immediate income, while the wage-paying job has retirement benefits. Even today, very few weavers establish bank accounts or develop savings plans for their retirement. Jewelry, saddles, and other valuables represent substantial "savings accounts" and can be pawned at trading posts for cash. By and large, Navajos expect children to care for their elderly parents. But even though she has five adult children, Yazzie seeks financial independence in her old age.

Will this innovator ever really quit weaving? Wrily, but perhaps realistically, she says she'll probably keep it up, "Just so I get the money, I guess."

Burntwater Rug 1984

Provenance: Steve Getzwiller,
Benson, Arizona, March 1984;
acquired March 1984

1984.61

Dimensions: 171.0 x 116.0 cm.
(67 x 46 in.)

Tapestry weave, dovetailed and diagonal
joins

Warp: handspun wool, z, natural white,
8/in.
Weft: handspun wool, z, natural and
vegetal colors, 50/in.
Selvage cords: warp—handspun wool,
3z-S, dark vegetal gold, 2-strand twining;
weft—handspun wool, 2z-S, light peach,
3-strand twining

19

Jennie Thomas

b. 1957

St. Michaels, Arizona

Clans: *Tábaahá* (water's edge people); *Tó dích'íi'nii* (bitter water people)

Jennie Thomas sold her first rug in 1976. Just out of high school, she wove in her mother's completely banded Wide Ruins style using yarns her mother had dyed. By the early 1980s, Thomas was winning prizes at the Gallup Inter-Tribal Indian Ceremonial and other competitions. Now an accomplished weaver in her mid thirties, Thomas is part of the new generation of young professionals who are redefining Navajo weaving. She has moved away from her family's Wide Ruins style and now uses Burntwater bordered patterns with small-scale detail and subtle pastel color changes. She has also woven rug-within-rug patterns, in which a banded Wide Ruins background is overlaid in the center with the design of a smaller, bordered Burntwater rug. Thomas often draws inspiration from Two Grey Hills and Ganado rugs and reworks their patterns in her mind until they fit her own aesthetic sense.

Thomas's extended family is well known for vegetal-dyed Wide Ruins

rugs. Thomas and her three sisters learned weaving from their mother, Betty B. Roan, who has rugs in many prominent collections. Thomas is also related by clan and marriage to the famous weavers and dyers of the Smith family of Wide Ruins, which includes Ellen, Agnes, and Mary Smith, Annie Tsosie, and Mary and Nellie Roan. The women all take considerable interest in one another's work, especially in who sold what to whom and for how much. Several of Thomas's relatives in Wide Ruins and Klagetoh spin wool and dye yarn, which she buys and uses alongside her own handspun yarns. Thomas has taught other women in her home community to weave and earn their own living. Her twelve-year-old daughter, Desiree, has not yet begun to weave but is already talking about which universities she wants to attend after high school. She'll be following in the footsteps of many college-educated cousins, aunts, and uncles.

Although she grew up in Wide Ruins, Thomas spent her own high school years in Utah with a Mormon foster family. For the past fourteen years, she and her family have lived on the outskirts of Window Rock in St. Michaels, where Desiree's father is an administrator for the tribal government. They live in a trailer home and make frequent weekend visits to their ranch 100 miles away in Pinon, where his family lives.

To get the highest prices for her weaving, Thomas travels to galleries such as Garland's in Sedona and Christof's in Santa Fe. "Sometimes," she says, "I have individual collectors who are interested in my rugs. I call them and tell them when one is ready, then I leave the decision up to them." Her standards are high: "I know how much I want for a rug when I make it. It depends on the work and how it looks. It takes a lot of work, a lot of my time to weave. It's a headache if I can't think of a

design. I have to sit there and concentrate and be patient. I don't think people realize how much time it takes!"

Burntwater Rug 1991

Provenance: Christof's, Santa Fe, New Mexico, 1991; acquired August 1991

1991.759

Dimensions: 110.5 x 77.0 cm. (44 x 30½ in.)

Tapestry weave, dovetailed joins

Warp: processed wool, z, natural white, 13/in.
Weft: Wilde & Woolly processed wool yarn, z, natural and vegetal colors, 80/in.
Selvage cords: handspun wool, handplied, 2z-S, dusty rose, 3- and 4-strand twining

20

Helen Bia

b. 1945

Three Turkey Ruins, Arizona

Clans: *Ta'neeszahnii* (tangle people);
born for *Ma'ii deeshgiizhnii* (coyote
pass people)

Helen Bia's extended family lives near Three Turkey Ruins in the backcountry between Chinle and Nazlini. For more than three decades, the weavers in this family have been known for their subtle combinations of vegetal-dyed creams, yellows, golds, oranges, and greens. Yellow and gold dyes are readily obtained from plants, and the Bia women are experts at creating distinctive shades of green, one of the toughest to create.

One of Helen Bia's rugs won Best of Show at the Heard Museum's Indian arts and crafts exhibition in 1974, and she has been winning prizes ever since. Initiated by Helen's mother, family matriarch Mary Bia, the Three Turkey Ruins style is now shared by Helen, her sisters Ruth Ann Tracey, Lucy Begay, and Alice B. Begay, her daughter Gloria, and her niece Irene. Their work combines the colors and simplicity of Chinle rugs with the Ganado/Two Grey Hills/Burntwater layout—a bordered pattern of one or two central diamonds, often stepped rather than serrated, with matching filler motifs. Because the style is a hybrid and the local trading post hasn't strongly promoted the area's rugs, the Three Turkey Ruins style is not well known.

Traders and museums are likely to type Bia family rugs as Burntwaters, especially since one of Helen Bia's rugs was published under the Burntwater category in the July 1974 *Arizona Highways*. But Three Turkey Ruins rugs have fewer colors and more symmetrical design elements than classic Burntwaters and a more consistent character than the newest, experimental Burntwater derivations. This raises a provocative question: How many independent styles woven by extended families have been overshadowed by regional styles and other widespread types?

The Bia family makes both large and small rugs. They usually take the small, bread-and-butter rugs into Ganado or Gallup and shop around for the best price. The large ones are almost always commissioned by buyers like Steve Getzwiller of Benson, Arizona, who often makes special design requests. Using their own dyes and designs, the weavers have produced superb, tightly woven rugs for Getzwiller. Recently, he has further suggested they move away from their family style for the sake of marketing: "I resisted changing their palette because I really like it. But I bought a lot of their rugs, and, once you have a trunkful, what can you do? Now they're doing Ganado, Teec Nos Pos, and Two Grey Hills for me." Still, Getzwiller acknowledges, the weavers maintain ultimate control over their products. "It's a slow, slow transition. I keep telling them, 'No golds, no greens,' but they keep slipping those colors into their rugs. They buy their yarn in Sanders but still use their own vegetal dyes. Those are what is pretty to them."

Indeed, Helen Bia continues to weave "what is pretty" to her. She and twenty-four-year-old Gloria set their looms up side by side in Bia's one-room frame house. Color-coordinated in turquoise and peach, with "Santa Fe style" fabric on the kitchen chairs, the room displays the same aesthetic sensibility as Bia's rugs. "I think about designs and colors a lot," she says. "When Steve asks for certain colors, I still put them in the way I like, to make a better design. We have a lot of trust in each other, I guess. I'm willing to make any kind of design, but I do what looks good to me."

Three Turkey Ruins Rug 1990

Provenance: Hubbell Trading Post, Ganado, Arizona; acquired June 1990

1992.175

Dimensions: 93.0 x 62.0 cm
(36½ x 25 in.)

Tapestry weave, interlocked joins

Warp: processed wool yarn, z, natural white, 10/in.
Weft: handspun and processed wool yarn, z, natural and vegetal colors, 54-60/in.
Selvage cords: processed wool yarn, handplied, 3z-S, olive green, 2-strand twining

21

Kalley Musial

b. 1953

Flagstaff, Arizona

Clans: *Tó díchʼíiʼnii* (bitter water people); born for *Tábaahá* (water's edge people)

An ambitious young artist, Kalley Musial challenges herself to interpret her personal feelings through the traditional medium of weaving. Musial says her rugs and wall hangings reflect her changing moods: one rug may be calm and soothing, another agitated or darkly brooding. If there is illness in the family, it shows in her work; if there is cause for celebration, that too shows. "Instead of getting upset, I spread out my colors, sit down at the loom, and see what comes out," she says. Because she wants to sustain the same feeling throughout a piece, Musial often takes an incomplete rug off the loom frame and stores it until she feels like returning to it; she often has four or five works in progress simultaneously.

Musial learned to weave from her mother, Carol Yazzie Keams, when she was six or seven, but she quit by the age of twelve as school increasingly absorbed her interests. After high school, she studied computer science at a local college. She didn't return to weaving until her mid twenties, when her daughter Jennie (22) was still a child. In part, she credits Colorado anthropologist Joe Ben Wheat for encouraging her to find a unique mode of expression: "He gave me a real boost. At that time I wasn't too excited about my weaving, and he kept saying it was really good." She says that Robert Breunig, then curator at the Museum of Northern Arizona and now director of the Desert Botanical Garden, "made me realize I had a responsibility to share my weaving through demonstration, lectures, and workshops."

In her recent work, Musial strives to express her feelings through her colors and keeps the designs relatively simple. Although she has made storm patterns and bordered designs with central motifs, Musial prefers all-over banded designs that allow her to work more with color. To achieve desired shades, she experiments widely with dyes. Her unusual results include a heathered salmon-pink she created on gray wool with a snakeweed dye and an aniline top-dye, a light green she made by putting an iron skillet into a rabbitbrush dye bath for several hours; and a light yellow she extracted from the marigolds in her garden.

Regarding herself as a fine artist, Musial is one of the few weavers who regularly titles rugs. Hers often reflect the moods or feelings that inspired the rug: *Black and Blue and Bruised All Over* is a "Moki" stripe she made when her daughter left home for the first time to attend boarding school. When Musial visited Japan in 1988, she wove a demonstration rug sardonically titled *Made in Japan*. She calls another rug *Cloudy Sunset* because "sunsets are a mixture of happiness and sadness to me," she says. "I try to get people to associate a scene with a feeling; titles help people understand why the colors came together."

When her Ross collection rug was still on the loom, Musial traveled to Maine for an exhibition at the University of Maine at Orono. "What I was feeling when I wove it was a lot of good feelings mixed with bad ones. I think that a lot of the rugs that I do represent both sides—difficult times and trying to bring back a balance. There were pressures: getting ready to go to Maine, showing them what I do with my work, and still trying to spend time with my family. And basically trying to balance two cultures—that's hard to do every day but especially when I travel." When she arrived in Maine, she discovered that the rug's colors were those of the New England autumn: "My colors were all around me!" Her trip "down east" is reflected in the rug's subtle melding of southwestern and autumnal eastern hues. The facetious pun in her title, *My Maine Rug*, suggests that every rug she produces is her "main" rug: "They are like children to me—each one individual and a part of me."

Musial combines weaving with a demanding schedule of teaching and demonstrations. The only Ross collection weaver who teaches regular classes for *bilagáana*, Musial has led beginning and advanced workshops at museums in Arizona, California, New York, and Maine. She also teaches two younger sisters, her daughter, and a niece. While guiding their technique, she leaves design and color choices strictly up to each individual.

In addition to the workshops, she has demonstrated for museums, galleries, and art festivals in Japan, in the Bahamas, and throughout the United States. Since these activities already take so much time away from her own weaving and her family life, she's had to turn down offers to demonstrate in Australia and China. During her travels, she carries a portable loom that can go wherever she goes.

Musial's biggest challenge in all these public activities is to deal with people who expect "the traditional Navajo woman from a hundred years ago" and who "want to weave just like in the old days." Even then, she emphasizes, weavers experimented with new materials, adapted to new situations, and combined traditional techniques with new designs to express themselves in unique ways. She hopes to break down the stereotype of Navajo weavers as older women living in rural isolation, constrained by local traditions.

Musial lives on the outskirts of Flagstaff with her daughter Jennie and son Lee. She regularly takes a booth at the annual Indian Market in Santa Fe and exhibits work at the Coconino Center for the Arts in Flagstaff. Since it's hard to keep enough of her work in stock to supply galleries, she maintains a long waiting list of customers. Those that finally purchase a rug receive one well worth waiting for.

My Maine Rug: The Colors of Autumn 1991

Provenance: Acquired February 1991

Exhibitions: *Beyond Tradition*, Oklahoma City, Oklahoma, November 1990

1991.702

Dimensions: 113.0 x 72.0 cm. (44 x 28½ in.)

Tapestry weave, interlocked joins

Warp: processed wool yarn, z, natural white, 10/in.
Weft: Wilde & Woolly processed wool yarn, z, natural, vegetal and aniline colors, 56/in.
Selvage cords: Wilde & Woolly processed wool yarn, handplied, 2z-S, light gray, 2-strand twining

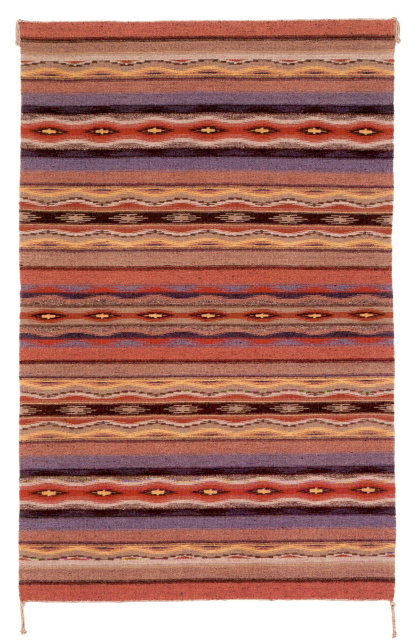

22

Jennifer Musial

b. 1976

Flagstaff, Arizona

Clan: *Tó díchʼíiʼnii* (bitter water people)

For this rug, fifteen-year-old Jennifer Musial won Best of the Juvenile Division and Best of Category at the 1991 Indian Market in Santa Fe. No newcomer to prizes, she had already earned blue ribbons at the same competition three years running. Still, the 1991 occasion—top prize in her division—was one to celebrate. "Each year I'd been excited, but this was bigger," she says. "When I first saw it, I didn't believe it. I was so excited. When I picked up the rug the next morning and it had three ribbons—wow! That was really neat. My mom was proud and that really meant something to me."

Both her mother, Kalley Musial (21), and grandmother, Carol Yazzie

Keams, trained Jenny in basic weaving techniques, but they always left the design up to her. Not surprisingly, her choice of banded designs and dusky colors closely resembles her mother's well-known expressionistic works. In fact, for this rug, Musial used yarns left over from one of her mother's projects. This is a common practice among young people just learning to weave.

Musial says weaving releases her from the pressures of school and growing up, but it also creates pressures of its own. She wove the Ross collection rug during a summer when she attended two sessions of volleyball camp and was about to enter a private boarding school in Pasadena, California. Like her mother, she sought to express her feelings through her weaving: "We always have a lot of colors [of yarn] around, but these are the ones I chose. They're kind of dark. I guess it's because I was leaving my family and old school and everything. I was leaving, and I didn't really want to let go. I'd just got out of school and I put that rug up [on the loom], and I had a bunch of other things to do along with getting ready for school [in Pasadena]. I didn't think I had enough time . . . and in the week between [volleyball camps] I just wove day and night. I didn't do anything else. Then when I came back from the second camp, I had three days before market, and I finished it. I had to time everything just perfectly, but I put everything I had into it—to do something good. I didn't do it to win, but to do it right.

"That rug was a lot more complicated than others I've done. It has three [bands of] designs on it— one in the middle and then one on each side of the middle. The squash design—the one with points—is one that I like to do. It's easier to do, and faster. The stepped designs on either side are cloud designs; that's what Mom's grandma called them."

On other rugs, Musial has collaborated with her maternal grandmother, Carol Yazzie Keams. They share the credit and income from their joint ventures. One of their early projects, *Young Meets Old*, was exhibited in 1988 at the Coconino Center for the Arts in Flagstaff. In a candid gallery label, Kalley Musial wrote, "Grandmother and granddaughter, equally stubborn in their beliefs, . . . create beauty through understanding and sharing." In this family, weaving provides a significant opportunity for contact between the generations, but minor points of contention still occur: when she isn't weaving, Jenny Musial likes to leave the loom uncovered in the living room so she can ponder the rug's design, but her grandmother prefers to keep it covered, in the traditional way.

Like other teens, Musial has lots of school-related activities—studies, sports, friendships—and weaving only fits into this busy schedule during the summer. She notes with pride that her high school is very strict. "I have hours of homework every night, but it's important because I want to get into a good college." For now, her plans include weaving only as a hobby: "I want to be a child pyschologist because I love kids. I want to help out other people, especially teenagers, because I've been there too."

Rug 1991

Provenance: Mr. and Mrs. Jeffrey M. Kahn, New York, August 1991; acquired as gift September 1991

Awards: Best of Juvenile Division and Best of Category, 1991 Indian Market, Santa Fe

1991.756

Dimensions: 62.0 x 38.0 cm. (25 x 15 in.)

Tapestry weave, interlocked joins

Warp: processed wool yarn, z, natural gray-white, 11/in.
Weft: Wilde & Woolly processed wool yarn, z, natural and vegetal colors, 60/in.
Selvage cords: processed wool yarn, handplied, 2z-S, black, 3-strand twining

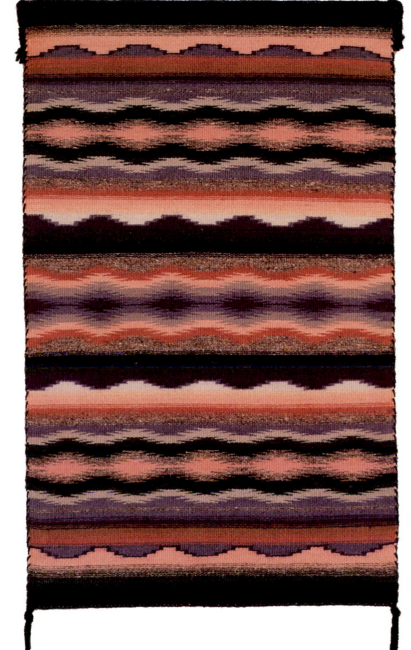

In their eclectic meld of old and new, pictorial rugs mirror contemporary Navajo life. Themes run the gamut from nostalgic to starkly modern, from secular to sacred. Images may be drawn from almost anywhere, isolated from their naturalistic context or made part of complex scenes. Humor abounds, and feelings find expression—horror at an ugly dam masking the landscape, delight in a hot air balloon show, love for a pet lamb.

While many different weavers use the same popular images, such as Monument Valley rock formations, each has a distinctive way of handling them. In the Ross collection's largest rug, Ason Yellowhair (23) takes images of plants and birds from the natural world, stylizes them, and freezes them in formal rows. Using a cartoonlike style that reduces her everyday subjects to basic geometric shapes, Susie Dale (24) treats the elements of Navajo life with playful humor. The weaver of the Ross collection's American flag rug (30) reveals a fascination with everyday icons, as well as the patriotic sentiment common among Navajos, especially those whose family members served in the armed forces.

Even mothers and daughters or sisters who weave together have unique pictorial styles. Each weaver of landscape scenes will make her hogans, corrals, plants, animals, wagons, and distant buttes according to a different, but internally consistent, plan. The way a weaver treats clouds is often a clue to her identity. Isabell John (25) weaves shallow, horizontally oriented semicircles in winter, which grow into billowing cumulus in her summer rugs. In contrast, another weaver's clouds almost always appear triangular with sharp points

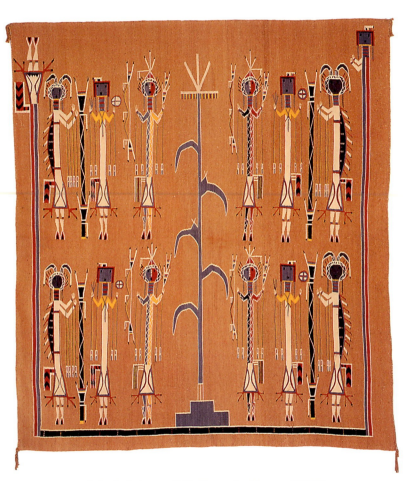

9. Sandpainting rug, 1940s. Denver Art Museum. 1950.185

(26). Susie Dale (24) makes minimalist clouds, barely squeezed in above her horizon lines.

Four weavers represented in the Ross collection approach religious subject matter in distinctive ways. Hoping to preserve something of Navajo culture for future generations, Isabell John depicts important moments of a religious yé'ii bicheii ceremony and its accompanying social activity in her large rug. Distancing herself from the ceremony itself, one weaver

invented a clever rug-within-rug format in which she shows two people holding up a pictorial rug that depicts yé'ii bicheii dancers performing. Another weaver (28) miniaturizes the yé'ii bicheii figures. Using motifs abstracted from sacred sandpaintings, Audrey Wilson (29) presents two yé'ii in the frontal, stylized fashion used by many other rug weavers; her distinctive variation is to make the rug two-faced and to add a fancy twill-block border.

Pictorial rugs with religious subjects do not serve as objects of devotion, nor do they attempt to represent religious narratives. Weavers consistently report that they think about both geometric and pictorial designs principally as decorative motifs: "Some ladies may know the signs, but I really don't know them," says one weaver of her geometric motifs. "It's just a design. I don't think my mother knew. If she knew, she'd tell me. But we don't know." Another woman explains, "It just gets into your mind, and you start out on your design."

Even when rugs contain religious motifs like *yé'ii* (holy people) or sandpainting designs (fig. 9), the rugs themselves are not generally used in religious ceremonies, nor are they considered intrinsically sacred. This lack of sacredness in the rugs' imagery contrasts deeply with the process of weaving which, at least for some people, still relates to religious beliefs and practices, retains symbolic significance in its tools and behaviors, and occasionally requires prayer, songs, and ritual performance.

There are traditional taboos against weaving certain images such as *yé'ii*, snakes, bears, horned toads, and butterflies into rugs, but today beliefs vary from family to family. Copies of sandpaintings used in healing rituals and certain other religious motifs are considered particularly dangerous by some. "It will do away with your eyesight." "My grandma told us not to do that because it would affect one of us. We might not be healthy when we grow older." "My sister did the *yé'ii bicheii* [in her rug], and she got sick because she didn't have any *yé'ii bicheii* [ceremony] done for her." Some weavers still dare to make such designs occasionally because they find them pretty or intriguing and, especially, because they sell extremely well. Most agree that in order to weave them safely, a special ceremony should be performed by a medicine man either before or after the rug is made: "Don't ever do it unless you have a sing done for it. Then you can do something like *yé'ii bicheii*."

23

Ason Yellowhair

b. 1930

Smoke Signal, Arizona

Clans: *Tó dích'íi'nii* (bitter water people); born for *Kiyaa'áanii* (towering house people)

"The land was filled with deer and covered with beautiful flowers. The air had the odor of pollen and fragrant blossoms. Birds of the most beautiful plumage were flying in the air, or perching on the flowers and building nests in the deer's antlers." So nineteenth century scholar Washington Matthews describes the setting for a Navajo legend in which a hero travels through enchanted lands (Reichard 1950:263). He might well have been traveling through the scenery of one of Ason Yellowhair's rugs.

Birds are important in traditional Navajo religion. The bluebird, for instance, is considered "the bird of dawn, of promise, and of happiness," and certain birds' songs "represent happiness, peace, and prosperity" (Reichard 1950:192, 256, 395-398). A sandpainting of the

Corn People for the Male Shootingway ceremony shows four holy figures with cornstalk bodies, each with a different colored bird atop his feather headdress (Wyman:pl. 22). Birds appear in many other sandpaintings, with and without plants. Although she knows they play a significant role in traditional religion, Yellowhair says the birds in her rugs carry no specific sacred meaning, tell no particular story, but simply express a positive and happy outlook on life.

Yellowhair moved from banded geometric designs in vegetal colors to pictorial rugs with stylized *yé'ii* figures in the 1950s and continued experimenting until her present style became popular with buyers in the 1970s. She says her original inspiration for bird and flower imagery came from her love of the outdoors, and, according to her daughter, Elsie T. Tom, she based the stylized plant forms on Wrigley's Spearmint Chewing Gum wrappers.

Rugs showing birds perched on cornstalks, trees, or unidentifiable leafless forms date from the early 1900s, but none contains the detail and variety of contemporary rugs. Only members of the extended Yellowhair family make bird-and-flower rugs in the distinctive Yellowhair style, which is characterized by a large, horizontal format, simple borders, and several rows of plants and birds running at right angles to the weaving direction. Families in the Gap and Cedar Ridge area of the western reservation and around Sanders in the southeast make a related style, equally detailed. These rugs usually have a vertical format showing colorful birds perched on a single tasseled cornstalk, often growing out of a shallow Navajo wedding basket.

Seven of Yellowhair's nine daughters and two daughters-in-law weave— Leita Y. Bedonie, Marta Y. Yazzie, Jane T. Nelson, Ella Mae Yellowhair,

Alice M. Yellowhair, Marilyn Y. Begay, Elsie T. Tom, Susie B. Yellowhair, and Darlene B. Yellowhair. Ason Yellowhair taught most of her daughters when each was about ten. "So," she says jokingly, "they could buy their own school clothes." Some of her grandchildren already know how to weave; many are still learning.

Large rugs are the Yellowhair family specialty. "If I want to work very hard, then I make a very large rug." Elsie T. Tom remembers helping her mother finish the final two inches of the Ross collection rug, a prodigious task because of its size, almost eleven by eight feet. The task took several days and, since a darning needle has to be pressed between the highly tensioned warps in order to insert the last wefts, was very hard on the fingers.

Ason is another way to spell *'Asdzáán*, Navajo for *woman, wife,* or *Mrs.* Though it is her given name and not a title, Ason's name translates as "Mrs. Yellowhair" or, in the old-fashioned way, "Old Lady Yellowhair." Accompanied only by a young grandson who helps with chores, she lives in an isolated area in a one-room hogan without modern amenities. Proud of being an independent woman, Yellowhair says it is much easier to weave without a man in the house: "When you put up a loom to weave, you're not supposed to put your arms around your man in front of the rug. It's dangerous to the rug. If you do this, then your rug won't be even on the edges."

She insists, too, that women's work is equal to men's in its demands and its contributions to a household. As she explains in Navajo, "See, a man might be making a house, and he gets very tired. It's like that weaving too—your back and your arms and your legs hurt. A man might work very hard on the railroad, and weaving is like doing the same kind

24

Susie Shirley Dale

b. 1931

Kinlichee, Arizona

Clans: *Tó díchʼiiʼnii* (bitter water people); born for *Maʼii deeshgiizhnii* (coyote pass people)

Susie Dale weaves nostalgic pastoral scenes of Navajo life as it often looked a few decades ago. In her Ross collection rug, she shows people herding sheep, loading a wagon, and sitting outside old-fashioned log hogans. Pickup trucks and wagons are parked amid cattle and sheep.

The Dale family compound sits on the edge of the Fort Defiance plateau amid piñon trees and scattered rock outcroppings like those in her picture. But today many of the houses in the compound are made of flat gray stucco or stone, with modern windows. Dale's three sons and six daughters, like many younger Navajos, drive compact cars more often than pickups, and they are away at school or jobs more often than working in the fields.

After she learned the basic and herringbone twill weaves by watching her mother, the eleven-year-old Dale never returned to school. She taught herself to make two-faced rugs by trial and error after watching a paternal aunt, Edith James, who is widely known for

excellent fancy weaving. Dale's mother makes vegetal-dyed rugs similar to the banded style from Chinle. Three of her four sisters also weave, but only a few of the next generation have yet learned.

The other weavers in Dale's extended family and in the surrounding community of Kinlichee almost all use geometric designs in their rugs. One of Dale's three sisters, Nellie Brown, makes vegetal-dyed rugs like her mother, Hasbah Shirley, in a style similar to the banded patterns associated with Chinle. Dale herself chooses to do scenes with animals and people because modestly sized pictorials generally bring more money than geometric patterns of the same dimensions. She also finds that a sequence of images gives her more opportunity for variety and humor than a single symmetrical design allows. Dale makes *yéʼii* pictorials as well—the only member of her family and community whose repertoire includes both rug types.

Dale's method of rendering the natural world is not unique, though it is unusual in her home area. Weavers from the Dinnehotso, Lukachukai, and Four Corners areas frequently make rugs in a similar style, with perspective indicated by a vertical progression and subjects intentionally abstracted to simple geometric shapes. Assessing Dale's Ross collection rug, a pictorial weaver from Lukachukai commented wryly, "So they have long cows, long sheep over there!"

After negotiating her price for this rug with trader Bill Malone, Dale took her payment in cash, groceries, and several cases of soft drinks—the standard form of payment for many decades. She and most of her family sell their rugs at Hubbell's and J. B. Tanner's at Ya-Ta-Hey, not just because these are the closest trading posts, but because they have built a relationship of trust with the traders over the years.

Pictorial Rug 1991

Provenance: Hubbell Trading Post, Ganado, Arizona, June 1991; acquired June 1991

1991.723

Dimensions: 127.0 x 76.0 cm. (50 x 30 in.)

Tapestry weave, interlocked joins

Warp: commercial wool yarn, 4z-S, natural white, 8/in.
Weft: handspun wool and processed wool yarn, z, natural, vegetal, and aniline colors, 36-44/in.
Selvage cords: warp—outer warps processed wool yarn, handplied, 3z-S, no twining; weft—handplied, 2z-S, gray-brown, 2-strand twining; braided corner tassels

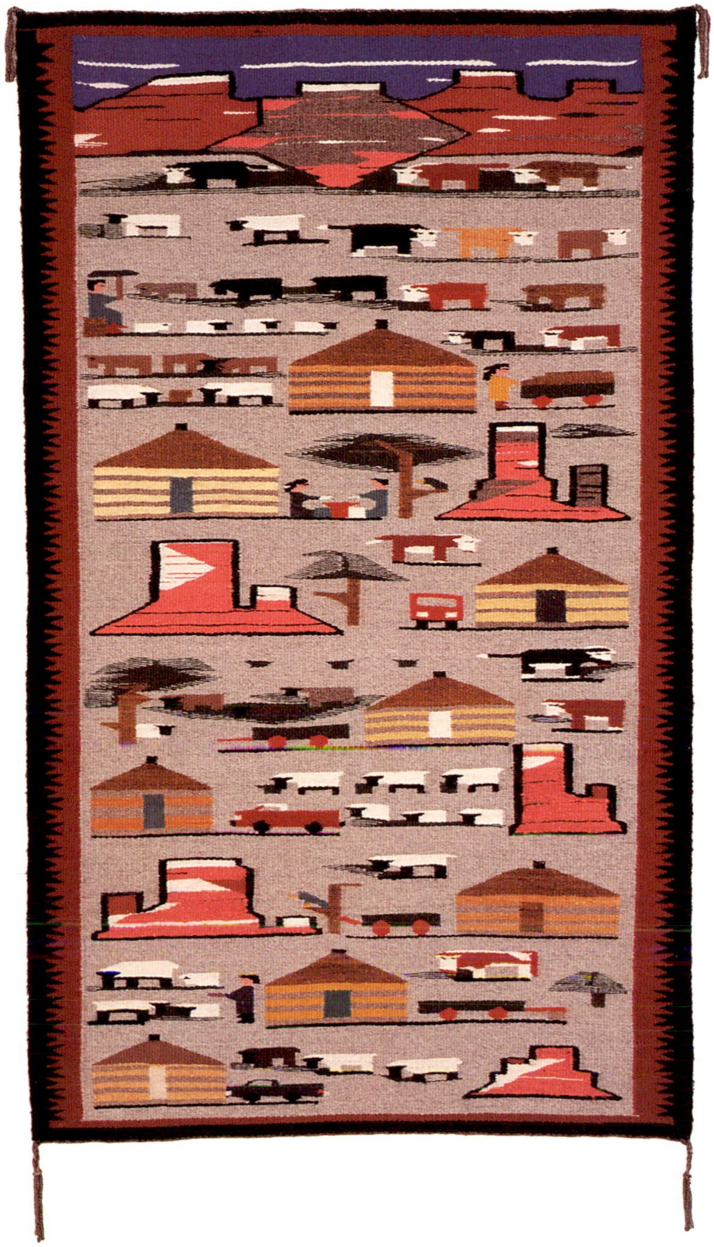

25
Isabell John

b. 1933

Many Farms, Arizona

Clans: *Tó dích'íi'nii* (bitter water people); born for *Áshiihí* (salt people)

Isabell John often weaves scenes setting forth her vision of traditional Navajo life. Her rugs show "the way I live—the hogan, the corrals, the livestock. *Dine'é baghan, dine'é be'iina'*—the Navajo philosophy of life, the way of life." These scenes, however, do not represent actual places. As her son Dennison explains, "She 'picturizes' the scene, sees it in her mind the way she wants to."

John has a particular mission in choosing these images. "Today," she explains through Dennison, who acts as her interpreter, "our younger generation doesn't know what our traditional ways are. They don't inherit our traditional ways. I see that we're losing our culture. These kids might lose it in the next generation. Every day on the Navajo Nation network radio, I hear them talk about traditional ways, saying we might lose our identity and our clan ways. Maybe these rugs will bring back the heritage of the *dine'é*.

Throughout the nation, we might identify with these rugs and these ceremonies."

John's Ross collection rug depicts a *yé'ii bicheii* ceremony, the traditional Night Chant, encircled by spectators' wagons. She says of it, "This is a traditional way of *dine'é* healing. It's a nine-day ceremony for the healing of a person." Two women bearing baskets greet a procession of male and female holy people, the sacred *yé'ii* of Navajo religion. Talking God, the *yé'ii bicheii* (grandfather of the *yé'ii*), is wrapped in a deerskin and leads the procession while a blue-shirted Water Sprinkler brings up the rear. John describes Water Sprinkler as "a funny man, always running around, acting like a clown." The scene shows the final night of the ceremony, the only night on which masked female dancers appear, according to John. Two bonfires burn as animals graze peacefully in the distance. The snow-capped peaks tell us it is winter, the only season when such ceremonies are held.

Isabell John's commitment to the Navajo pastoral tradition has been lifelong. She attended Chinle Boarding School until third grade, when, because "there were sheep, and there were horses, and there were cattle to take care of," her father took her out of school to work at home. She learned to weave at about eight, and her father died five years later. By then, she had already discovered that "when you have livestock, then you can make a living."

Through the 1950s and 1960s, Isabell John's family and neighbors made *yé'ii* rugs, as well as the geometric patterns she calls "regular designs." In those days, they all took their rugs to nearby trading posts where they exchanged them for groceries and supplies. Today the posts at Many Farms, Lukachukai, Upper Greasewood, and Dinnehotso where the family once traded are closed, some replaced by fast food

restaurants and gas stations and others by vacant lots. Following the trend in modern marketing, John sells now to galleries in Durango and Sedona and to free-lance rug merchants, and her rugs are often featured in slick color advertisements in southwestern arts magazines. In collaboration with Toh Atin Gallery in Durango, Colorado, she authorized a limited edition serigraph reproducing a pastoral scene from one of her rugs, a blue-ribbon winner at the 1981 Gallup Inter-Tribal Indian Ceremonial.

In the early 1970s, John became the first in her immediate area to put people, animals, and landscapes into her rugs. Her example was quickly taken up by others. Some learned directly from her; others simply borrowed ideas. A decade later she began weaving her initials and the date into some of her rugs, but by then there was little need. John's pictorial style, with its superb workmanship and large scale, is easy to differentiate from imitators.

While she continues to weave favorite scenes like the *yé'ii bicheii* ceremony, John keeps trying to create fresh images that will appeal to buyers because, as she explains, "There's money involved, too. It's for income to support the family." She has depicted squaw dances and a nighttime fire dance. Both she and her daughter-in-law, Geanita John, have made rugs showing the back view of a single weaver seated at her loom—in Isabell's case, sometimes nearly life-size self-portraits. She also weaves sandpainting rugs on special order, but only after consulting one of the medicine men in her family. Although John and some of the family are also members of the Native American Church, she has not used imagery from peyote prayer meetings in her work.

Isabell John and her husband, Frank, live in a handsome, one-room hogan many miles off the pavement. There, like her parents and grandparents,

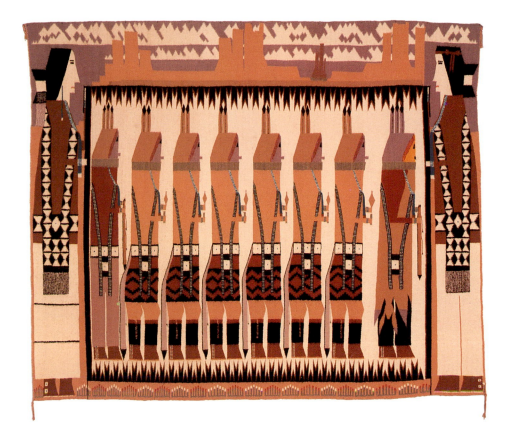

Anonymous[1]

Navajo Reservation, Arizona

It took the weaver seventeen months of steady work just to weave this "superfine" tapestry after months spent preparing the handspun yarn. Although she occasionally weaves other designs such as sandpaintings and simpler *yé'ii bicheii* tapestries (27), her favorite image is a pictorial rug-within-rug. Her daughter weaves a variety of *yé'ii bicheii* rugs, including miniatures (28).

In this tapestry, a man and woman hold up a rug showing six masked male dancers—the holy people, or *yé'ii*. The dancers are led by Talking God, the *yé'ii bicheii* (grandfather of the gods) from whom the dance

takes its name, and followed by the Water Sprinkler. The two large figures wear traditional clothing, with turquoise necklace, concho belt, and concho-decorated medicine pouch. Their hair is tied into yarn-wrapped *tsiiyéél* (hair knots), the woman's decorated with white fringe. The dancers also wear concho belts and pouches; their kilts have identical patterns; and each dancer carries a rattle and prayer stick. Talking God is wrapped in a deerskin, and he and the Water Sprinkler both carry fox skins. Meadow flowers grow in the foreground at the rug bearers' feet, while behind the pictured rug cumulus clouds rise above sandstone spires that resemble those near the weaver's home. The angular clouds floating across a purplish-gray sky are one of her trademarks.

[1] For reasons of privacy, this weaver and her daughter have requested anonymity.

Yé'ii Bicheii **Rug-within-Rug** 1991

Provenance: Garland's Navajo Rugs, Sedona, Arizona; acquired October 1991

1991.835

Dimensions: 90.0 x 109.0 cm. (35½ x 43 in.)

Tapestry weave, interlocked and dovetailed joins

Warp: handspun wool, z, natural white, 16/in.
Weft: handspun wool, z, natural, vegetal and aniline colors, 96/in.
Selvage cords: handspun wool, handplied, 2z-S and 3z-S, tan and brown, 2-strand twining
Note: image woven at right angle to warp

they still raise sheep and cattle.
Photos of their four sons and three
daughters and many grandchildren
hang on the hogan walls, alongside
pictures of her prize–winning rugs.
While her children have jobs in
town, live in trailers and tract homes,
and enjoy modern conveniences,
John holds onto the traditional
Navajo way of life and hopes that her
grandchildren will someday learn
from her. As her pictorial rugs grow
on the large loom that dominates the
room, she sees them as powerful
teaching tools.

Yé'ii Bicheii Pictorial Rug 1982

Provenance: Toh Atin Gallery,
Durango, Colorado; acquired March
1982

1982.8

Dimensions: 122.0 x 211.0 cm.
(47½ x 83½ in.)

Tapestry weave, interlocked and
dovetailed joins

Warp: commercial wool yarn, respun,
4z-S, natural white, 11/in.
Weft: processed wool yarn, z, many
aniline and a few natural and vegetal
colors, 32/in.; commercial wool yarn,
4z-S, many aniline colors, 32/in.
Selvage cords: processed wool yarn,
handplied, 2z-S, aniline brown, 2-strand
twining

27

Anonymous

Navajo Reservation, Arizona

Miniature *Yé'ii Bicheii* Rug 1984

Provenance: Acquired 1984

1990.268

Dimensions: 27.5 x 27.0 cm.
(10¾ x 10½ in.)

Tapestry weave, interlocking and
dovetailed joins

Warp: handspun wool, z, natural white,
13/in.
Weft: handspun wool, z, natural, vegetal
and aniline colors, 98/in.
Selvage cords: handspun wool yarn,
handplied, 2z-S and 3z-S, black, 2-strand
twining
Note: image woven at right angle to warp

28

Anonymous

Navajo Reservation, Arizona

Miniature *Yé'ii Bicheii* Rug 1984

Provenance: Acquired 1984

1990.267

Dimensions: 8.5 x 11.4 cm.
(3½ x 4½ in.)

Tapestry weave, interlocking and
dovetailed joins

Warp: handspun wool, z, natural white,
16/in.
Weft: handspun wool, z, natural, vegetal
and aniline colors, 80/in.
Selvage cords: handspun wool yarn,
handplied, 2z-S and 3z-S, tan and brown,
2-strand twining
Note: image woven at right angle to warp

29

Audrey Spencer Wilson

b. 1920

Indian Wells, Arizona

Clans: *Tó dích'íi'nii* (bitter water people); born for *Ma'ii deeshgiizhnii* (coyote pass people)

T his textile shows Audrey Wilson's versatility in technique as well as design (13). One side is pictorial, the other entirely geometric. "This is the hardest to make" Wilson says. "You have to think hard to get that design in the back and then put your regular design on the front. You have to get it all the same size. You have to count all the strings in order to get it right." She calls this a "double weave in two faces rug" in English, "*alne'iistlóní*" in Navajo. The technique is commonly dubbed "double weave" by traders and collectors; the center design panel is technically a two-faced complementary weave structure with 3/1 interlacing (Emery 1966:153-154), and the border is a variation of diamond twill weave.

Wilson learned basic rug weaving from her mother before being sent away to school when her mother died. After leaving school, Wilson says, "I just got it into my mind what I wanted to weave. I started weaving and practiced, practiced, practiced. My first one was a really terrible weaving. My brother used to tell me, 'Make another one so I can

go down to the store and trade it and get you a candy.' . . . When I was a little girl I used to weave [plain stripes] all the time. That's the only way that I could go faster." As practice began to pay off, Wilson experimented with different weaves, including unusual variations of diamond twills, a method for making round rugs, and the two-faced weave shown here.

In many of her works, Wilson depicts elements of the traditional Navajo religion she has always practiced. Her father, H. Birch Spencer, was a prominent medicine man. She says, "Holy people are a main part of our Navajo way. I've got my own prayer and my own religion that I use. When I start [weaving], I just go ahead and start, but I pray in my religious way at the end. That's what my grandma told me, and my grandpa told me, too." She prefers to keep such rituals to herself and has not shared them with others. Like many Navajos, Wilson also regularly attends Christian services at a neighboring church and easily alternates between the two religions.

This rug does not tell a religious story or represent a specific sandpainting. Instead, like many *yé'ii* rugs, it combines motifs from Navajo sacred imagery into an appealing artistic composition without invoking specific religious beliefs. Despite the use of powerful Navajo symbols, *yé'ii* rugs have never had ceremonial functions; they are commercial products made to be sold to non-Indians. The central panel of this rug contains two stylized *yé'ii* figures, each wearing a feather, earrings and necklace, body paint, fringed sash, kilt, garters, and moccasins. Lightning lines, symbols of power, radiate from their kilt hems. Three large triangular objects with feather streamers and tassels form the center design. The figures are separated from the center by two columns of seven "sundogs" representing segments of rainbows (prisms) that are often seen near the

sun as light shines through ice crystals in the clouds.

When one of Wilson's two-faced *yé'ii* rugs appeared in a 1974 issue of *Arizona Highways* (1974:27) after winning Best of Show at the Gallup Inter-Tribal Indian Ceremonial that year, it sparked a spate of special orders from collectors and traders. Since then, she is kept so busy that she jokes about not recognizing her own rugs. "I read my name [on the tags]; that's the only way I could find mine." Still, many collectors readily recognize her work. The Ross collection rug was one of four or five that she wove in the same style during 1987-1988 and sold to J. B. Tanner's post just outside Gallup, almost three hours from her home. Still part of the old-fashioned trading system, Wilson receives jewelry and other goods, as well as cash, for her work.

On marketing, she comments, "Sometimes I go around when I finish my weaving. I go around to some people, some traders, who want to buy rugs. They ask me how much the price is. I always set my price high. The reason why I do that is because I don't use a pattern, I use my head. White people do it that way too—they use their heads, and then they want their prices high too. That's the way with mine."

Painful arthritis has begun to limit Wilson's weaving in recent years. "I used to card and dye my own wool, but I don't do it anymore. I buy it now. That's the only way I can do it now, because it's getting hard for me—arthritis in both hands, my elbows, my knees." Widowed twice and mother of three grown sons, Wilson has shared her modest two-room house with an older brother for many years. From their isolated home, one can "see forever" across the windswept grasslands, dotted with herds of sheep and cattle, the Hopi Buttes in the distance. In the dim light of the small weaving shed, another timeless vista: painstakingly woven *yé'ii* emerge from Wilson's giant loom.

Yé'ii Two-Faced Rug 1988

Provenance: J. B. Tanner Trading Company, Ya-Ta-Hey, New Mexico; consigned to Indian Trader West, Santa Fe, New Mexico; acquired August 1988

1988.120

Dimensions: 154.5 x 130.0 cm. (61 x 50½ in.)

Two-faced tapestry weave, diagonal joins, and 3-color weft-faced diamond twill weave

Warp: processed wool, z, natural white, 12/in.
Weft: processed wool yarn and handspun wool, z, natural, aniline and vegetal colors, 12/in. on each face
Selvage cords: processed or handspun wool, 2z-S, aniline top-dyed black, 2-strand twining
Note: image woven at right angle to warp

30

Attributed to Mary Gould

Location unknown

The Stars and Stripes are not new to Navajo weavers. In an 1873 photograph, a Navajo woman sits beside a small, partially completed rug with a U. S. flag motif while New Mexico Governor W. F. M. Arny looks on (Amsden 1934:pl. 114; after Pepper 1923). More than a hundred years later, the flag idea endures. In July of the Bicentennial year, Sadie Curtis was shown on the cover of *Arizona Highways* magazine with a nearly finished American flag rug she was weaving to benefit a scholarship fund at the Navajo Community College in Tsaile. Mary Lee Begay wove a huge Arizona state flag rug for the same project (*Arizona Highways* 1976:cover, 14-15). Curtis has since made others on commission and used the theme again for her youngest son's high school graduation present in 1989.

The weaver of this U. S. flag in the Ross collection remains a mystery. Two Mary Goulds—Mary Louise and Mary Joe—live near each other in the Two Grey Hills community, and both are known for fine rugs of natural-colored wools. But neither of them recalls making this rug, and its weaver remains unidentified.

Systematically recording weavers' names and communities is a relatively new practice, begun only in the last three or four decades. Before that, weavers' names, especially their old-style Navajo names, were occasionally associated with a rug, but most artisans remained anonymous and some actually preferred it that way. According to Navajo custom, it is impolite to ask someone's name or to address people by name, because of the power naming holds. Using someone's name becomes a rude invasion of privacy. Instead, Navajos often use indirect designations, not only for those they are addressing, but for people they are talking about—usually kin terms like "Yazzie's brother" and descriptive names like "Tall woman with many notebooks."

In recent years, only a few weavers still prefer anonymity; most are pleased to be known for their work and realize that their name may help sell their rugs. "I don't care if you're going to use my name. I think it's better that way, that people know I'm weaving, how I weave." On rare occasions, trading posts put false names on rug tags when the weaver is unknown or a weaver requests her name be withheld. In the case of "Mary Gould," we do not yet know whether the name correctly identifies the weaver or whether some recordkeeping error has occurred.

United States Flag Rug about 1986

Provenance: Museum of Northern Arizona Gift Shop; acquired July 1986

Exhibitions: *37th Annual Navajo Show*, Museum of Northern Arizona, July 1986

1986.113

Dimensions: 206.5 x 148.0 cm. (82 x 58½ in.)

Tapestry weave, diagonal and interlocked joins

Warp: commercial wool yarn, 4z-S, natural white, 8/in.
Weft: processed wool yarn, z, dark aniline red, natural white, aniline blue, 28/in.
Selvage cords: commercial wool yarn, 2(4z-S), natural white, 2-strand twining
Note: prominent lazy lines

Why make a round or cross-shaped rug? Navajo weavers face the same aesthetic challenges and economic pressures as other contemporary artists. Finding an unusual shape or texture for a rug may solve a specific technical or aesthetic problem, and it may help bring the artist to the attention of buyers. Weavers find, though, that they must constantly temper experimentation with tradition. Rug buyers are willing to follow the artist on a new course only so long as the product still looks "Navajo."

Rose Owens (34, 35) is one of fewer than two dozen weavers who make round rugs. Her specialties include two-faced, diamond twill weave, and Ganado Red patterns. Alice Begay (36), like her grandmother before her, weaves cross-shaped rugs. She, too, frequently uses the Ganado Red style for her rugs, which are sometimes used as table covers, sometimes as wall hangings. Both of these women find that weaving oddly-shaped rugs keeps them from being bored and helps them build a reputation.

Amy Begay (31) makes tufting a compelling aesthetic feature by updating an old but rare style passed down in her family. Thick, tufted rugs were once woven as curios or as padding to cushion horse saddles, but Begay's version, too large to use as a saddle blanket, is made for looking at and touching. An aggressive marketer, Begay shows her large wall hangings at museum craft shows and sells flashy tufted dance leggings at powwows and other Indian gatherings.

Navajo weavers' interest in creating the illusion of depth with flat shapes and color contrast alone is at least as old as nineteenth century chief blankets, and the stacked boxes design, which plays with figure/ground ambiguity, frequently appears on modest double saddle blankets. In meeting a challenge from a friend who doubted she could even weave, occasional weaver Mary Brown (32) adapts this optical illusion to an extraordinary truck seat cover by nearly doubling its usual size. She approached the Ross collection when her friend pronounced the rug "too good to sit on."

Despite their durability and appealing appearance, twill and two-faced weaves are quite hard to find today because weavers know they don't command a high enough price to justify the work they require. Irene Julia Nez (33) ignores this advice because she likes the challenges of these difficult weaves, and she and her family have gained a reputation for combining the two.

The raised outline technique involves alternating two different colors of weft yarns in an otherwise normal tapestry weave. This alternation creates a background of pinstripes that seem to vibrate. Whenever the design dictates a change of colors, the wefts must float over two warps (instead of over one and under the next, as is usual) to preserve the striped background. By skipping over two warps, the wefts create a raised outline around each design element. The earliest known examples of this weave date to the mid 1930s.[1] Lillie Walker's roughly spun raised outline (37) is a modern extension of these.

Raised outlines reappeared in Coal Mine Mesa in the late 1950s, when Ned Hatathli encouraged area weavers to use the technique and promoted it as a regional style.[2] In the late 1960s, weavers began making raised outline rugs with more refined colors and elaborate designs borrowed from other styles. Recently, when many Coal Mine Mesa families relocated near Sanders, Arizona, local trader Bruce Burnham began promoting what he calls the "Newlands" style, raised outlines combined with smooth commercial yarns, vegetal pastels, and intricate patterns. Larry Yazzie (38) and his extended family weave subtly colored rugs that show the evolving nature of the raised outline today.

[1] I know of only three examples from the 1930s. One was acquired between 1937 and 1938 by John and Clara Lee Tanner (personal communication, 1977); the other two are in the collections of the Museum of Northern Arizona (785/E136, acquired 1934) and the California Academy of Science (370-680, acquired 1935).

[2] Maxwell (1963:46–47) credits the initial development of the technique to Hatathli (former Navajo Tribal Council member from the western reservation and founding president of Navajo Community College), but this is unlikely.

Round rug (35), Rose Owens, 1981. See p. 99.

31

Amy Begay

b. 1965

Chinle, Arizona

Clans: *Ta'neeszahnii* (tangle people); born for *Áshiihí* (salt people)

Amy Begay's tufted rugs regularly take prizes in the Novelty Weave category at the Museum of Northern Arizona's annual Navajo Show. With a clear marketing strategy mapped out, Begay plans to increase her prices steadily each year, as her proficiency increases and she becomes better known.

Tufted rugs are normally single or double saddle blanket size (thirty inches square or thirty by sixty inches). But Begay always wanted to make a much bigger one, and a Ross collection commission gave her the perfect opportunity. When her mother, Elsie Nez, saw the ambitious plans, she laughed and said, "Too big!"

Begay started the rug in early spring at shearing time, when she could select two large fleeces from Nez's goats. Nez usually sets aside just enough for the family's production of small rugs and sells the rest immediately. Finding someone else who hadn't already sold their mohair, an important cash crop, would have been a challenge.

Begay spent two full days washing the mohair she would later use for tufts. Over the next three weeks, she carded and spun the sheep wool she would use for the wefts and warps. The soft, plum-colored yarn in this rug is a commercial brand Begay buys from the Thunderbird Lodge shop at the mouth of Canyon de Chelly and the nearby tribal wool warehouse in Chinle. The weaving took seven or eight weeks. Begay wove only when her two young sons were asleep or when her husband or another relative could babysit.

Begay and Nez are among only ten or so women who still weave old-style tufted rugs. Begay learned the technique from Nez at ten. "She taught me a lot about weaving, which I'm very thankful for, especially because I can get money from it. When I was small, she used to tell me to weave because 'when you get a husband, then you'll know what to do.' Even though my husband has a good teaching job, I like to do what I can for our family income."

Every summer, Begay and her husband, Hanson, move from the Chinle area to Flagstaff to attend classes at Northern Arizona University, where Begay is working toward a degree in early childhood education and special education and Hanson is studying school administration. They share babysitting duties during classes. "My husband is my big support," Begay says. "He encourages me to do the tufted rugs. Sometimes he takes the kids out when I'm weaving. And he'll bring back yarn from the store for me when I need it, even though he gets embarrassed when he thinks the shopladies are looking at him as though he's buying it for himself!"

Begay says her family is constantly trying "to make different things that other people aren't always doing." Her pitch-coated basketry has won a prize at the annual Navajo Show, and her mother makes ceramic figurines and experiments with other crafts. "She's almost sixty and is a traditional woman," Begay says with admiration. "She doesn't work [outside the home] but takes care of one of my sisters' babies."

Around 1980, Begay's father, Ashinnie Nez, began crafting full-size and slightly smaller stuffed goats by mounting real goatskins and horns on wooden armatures. His realistic animals are now in popular demand by decorators, window dressers, and retail stores across the country. Through a relative in the Shonto area, he became interested in Navajo pottery; now he makes and sells his own. He also makes small loom frames on which Begay's mother weaves the beginnings of miniature rugs for displays. "He's a very hard-working man, supporting his family with everything he does," says Begay. "Most of his work goes to sending his daughters to school."

Tufted Rug 1989

Provenance: Acquired June 1989

1989.118

Dimensions: 196.5 x 99.5 cm. (77 x 39½ in.)

Weft-faced plain weave, with tufts of mohair inserted as supplementary pile wefts

Warp: handspun wool, z, natural white, 7/in.
Weft: handspun wool, z, natural white; processed wool yarn, z, aniline and blended gray, 40/in.; unspun mohair tufts, natural white, 2 rows/in.
Selvage cords: warp—handspun, 2z-S, natural white, 2-strand twining; weft— paired outer warps, no twining

32

Mary Brown

b. 1950

Phoenix, Arizona

Clan: *Ta'neeszahnii* (tangle people), born for *Kiyaa'áanii* (towering house people)

After fifteen years away from the loom, Mary Brown wove this rug when a friend challenged her to make a seat cover for his pickup. "He'd never seen me weave, so he said he didn't think I could. But after I started out, he kept saying, 'Oh, it's going up! You *do* know how to do it.'" Because she lives in Phoenix, Brown asked her mother, who lives in the family home at Pinon, to set up the loom and buy the yarn for her on the reservation. Once she started to weave back in Phoenix, Brown found she hadn't forgotten the basics. "I got the hang of it quickly," she says.

She spent several months weaving the rug on weekends and weekday afternoons after her job at the state highway department print shop. When her friend decided it was too good for his pickup, she sold the rug to the Ross collection with the help of a *bilagáana* friend in Phoenix and used the money to help pay for a religious ceremony for her son-in-law.

Brown has lived in Phoenix for twelve years but still goes home to the reservation to visit relatives and

attend ceremonies. She made sure her daughter spent some of her formative years on the reservation, too. "We sent her back up there because of her language. We wanted her to learn some Navajo traditional ways, so we sent her back up there when she was in tenth grade." Now, she is raising her own daughter on the reservation.

The only "occasional" weaver represented in the Ross collection, Brown is also one of the few who live off-reservation. Most occasional weavers simply are not proficient enough to make major pieces. What makes this rug exceptional is the control exercised over so many small, interrelated motifs in such a large format.

The "stacked boxes" pattern is often used for small, rough saddle blankets and throw rugs. Its optical effect exemplifies the Navajos' fascination with figure/ground ambiguity. For more than a century, weavers have created the illusion of depth in chief blankets in which a "background" of stripes is "overlaid" with a series of triangles and diamonds (1). In rugs of this century, adjacent color areas often appear to overlap; foregrounds emerge and backgrounds recede simply through the juxtaposition of solid shapes, without the use of shading or other perspective devices.

Brown is accustomed to being around innovators. Her grandmother made unusual round rugs with bird designs. The mother of the friend who prompted this rug once wove a highly unusual design inspired by crossword puzzles—"It didn't have the numbers, just the black and white squares."

Would she wait another fifteen years before weaving again? "I'll do another one, one of these days," was Brown's casual answer just after selling this rug. But in the six months that followed, she wove at least four more.

Stacked Boxes
Optical Illusion Rug 1991

Provenance: Acquired August 1991

1991.744

Dimensions: 188.0 x 114.5 cm. (36 x 24½ in.)

Tapestry weave, interlocked joins

Warp: processed wool yarn, z, natural white, 7/in.
Weft: processed wool yarn, z, natural and pre-dyed aniline colors, 10/in.
Selvage cords: warp—handspun wool, handplied, 2z-S, natural white, 2-strand twining; weft—plain

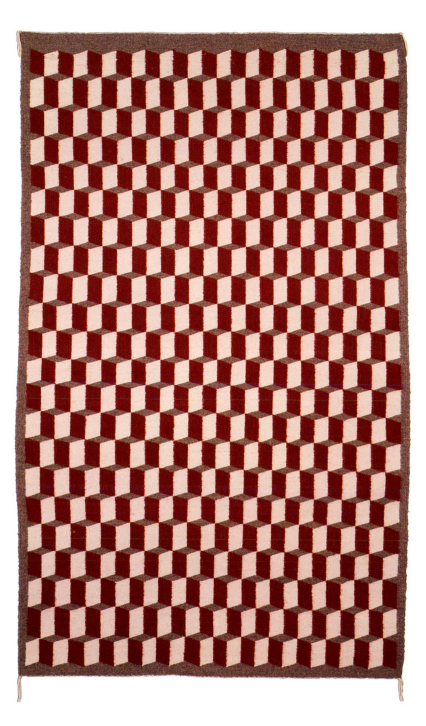

33

Irene Julia Nez

b. 1928

Kinlichee, Arizona

Clans: *Ma'ii deeshgiizhnii* (coyote pass people); born for *Tl'ízí láni* (many goats people)

Irene Julia Nez thinks tapestry weaves are harder to make than twill weaves like this, because they require "more thinking" about design. But both offer challenges and take careful planning. First, there are the basic materials: "When you make a rug of this size, you have to know how much yarn you're going to dye, how much white and gray to use, how many balls of yarn you need." The tapestry technique requires frequent changing of the yarns: "You have to break the yarn and then put another one in, and then you have all these strings hanging down." For twills, on the other hand, "You have to count the strings, and that's the hard part. Then, [to create an all-over series of diamonds or lozenges] you have three colors—that's all you can use."

Twills are just one of many rug types in Irene Nez's repertoire. She saw her first two-faced rug in 1946 at a rodeo. "I went home and tried and tried to count the threads like that. It took me three days to figure it out!" she recalls. Nez and her mother, Edith James, along with neighboring relatives like Dorothy Wilson, Desbah Evans, and Marie Begay, became well known for combining the two-faced technique with their already well-practiced diamond-twill weaves. By the early 1960s, even Nez's teenage sisters were winning top prizes at Arizona State and Navajo Tribal fairs for their two-faced/twill-weave combinations. The market value of these rugs declined through the seventies and eighties, but Nez's family kept making them. Nez's eighty-seven-year-old mother still weaves them today.

The thunderbird design on a cross-stitched tea towel inspired one of Nez's tapestry weave rugs. She changed the color scheme by substituting her own vegetal-dyed yellow for the original turquoise background. The bird's proportions also changed to fit the shape of her rug. "If I'm going to try to copy a picture, it won't come out exactly the way it looks. It's probably not going to be exactly the same."

Nez describes her approach to designing: "When you're just learning, you don't put fancy designs in. Then when you [are experienced enough to] really think about it, you can . . . . They just come to you, you know. You have this yarn and you see it and you will be thinking, 'Where shall I put this one?' Then, you just put it there. And then, from there on, you know it. It seems like it just comes to you. And if you don't like it, you can take it back out."

Twill-Woven Rug 1992

Provenance: Acquired 1992

1992.176

Dimensions: 181.0 x 114.0 cm. (72½ x 45½ in.)

Weft-faced diamond twill weave, 3-color sequence

Warp: processed wool yarn, z, natural white, 8/in.
Weft: processed wool yarn, z, natural white, aniline black and blended gray, 30/in.
Selvage cords: processed wool yarn, handplied, 2z-S, aniline black, red, and maroon, 3-strand twining

34

Rose Owens

b. 1929

Cross Canyon, Arizona

Clans: *Honágháahnii* (he walks around one people); born for *Deeschii'nii* (start of the red streak people)

Fewer than two dozen weavers make round rugs, and Rose Owens is one of the best. Although Ganado Red is her mainstay, she makes round rugs in other regional styles, as well as twill and two-faced weaves. Acquired by Gloria Ross for her personal collection and subsequently donated to the Denver Art Museum, this rug is a Ganado Red modified with pictorial elements.

Owens describes how, more than forty years ago, the idea to weave round rugs came to her. While herding sheep one early morning, she saw spider webs laden with dew, sparkling in the sunlight. The perfect geometry of the webs and the rainbow prisms gleaming from the dewdrops attracted her. She remembered that her father, a medicine man, once told her to rub spider webs on her face and hands

and pray that she could weave like the spiders. She also recalled the legend of Spider Woman, who taught weaving to the first Navajos when they emerged into the world. Inspired, Owens vowed to make round rugs. Her initial attempts were awkward and misshapen, but one day her husband brought her the perfect frame—a metal wagon wheel rim. She has made round rugs ever since. To this day, she has kept her methods secret to prevent other weavers from copying her.

This versatile and adventurous weaver's repertoire also includes full-scale chief blankets, rectangular Ganado Red and vegetal-dyed rugs, experimental patterns, and even old-fashioned twill saddle blankets. She weaves special orders for buyers across the country, including Gloria Ross, for whom she made several tapestries based on designs by contemporary painter Kenneth Noland. Recently, after another weaver failed, Owens wove a pictorial rug featuring an elaborate Fraternal Order of Police insignia for a benefit raffle.

Weaving contributes substantially to the Owens family income, but it means more than just cash to the weaver and her family. Owens invests herself in her weaving. When she sells a rug, she feels like she's selling a part of herself. "When you go to sleep, weaving is what you want to get up for the next day. If you don't weave, it's unhealthy to the mind. You get fat and lose your health. You get lazy. . . . You should be strong and healthy, feeling good. It's not how you feel just when you weave, but how you feel all day. If you're strong and brave enough, you still want to do things. If you're weak, you'll just be sitting there, not doing anything."

The traditional Navajo wedding basket, encircled by terraced black triangles, is an important image in some of Owens's rugs. In this rug, shallow basketry bowls are pictured

in profile at the top and bottom. Stylized feathers emerge from each basket, a reference to the Navajo fire dance, in which feathers seem to float or dance inside a basket. Owens makes actual baskets too, as well as traditional dresses, sash belts, moccasins, and knitted socks.

An expert herbalist, Owens is often consulted for her knowledge of local plants. She has a deep respect for traditional Navajo ways and likens herself to a university professor in the extent and significance of her knowledge. But, she notes with a chuckle, "I don't need books to remember what I know." She is active in community affairs and serves on the Kinlichee Chapter's school board and works with a group that helps the elderly.

Owens and her husband, Robert, neither of whom speaks English, provide traditional anchors for their family, but their children are taking widely divergent paths. The eldest son works in Window Rock for the tribal government; others have worked for the tribal forestry division, in construction, and at home managing livestock. Five of the six daughters are married with children, and all six have held jobs, such as welder-boilermaker trainee, hospital aide, school cafeteria cook, teacher's aide, ceramics instructor, and speech therapist. Two daughters and two granddaughters have attended college.

Only one of Owens's daughters weaves regularly, although each of them tried at least once to make a small rug before putting the loom aside. None of her granddaughters currently weaves, but Owens hopes some will take it up. "Of course," she emphasizes, "that is up to them if they want to learn. They can ask me when they're ready."

34

**Round Rug
with Baskets and Feathers** 1982

(illus. above)

Provenance: Gloria F. Ross, 1982;
acquired 1990

1990.270

Dimensions: diameter 109.0 cm. (43 in.)

Tapestry weave, interlocked joins

Warp: processed wool yarn, z, natural
white, 9/in.
Weft: processed wool yarn, z, natural and
pre-dyed aniline colors, 32-48/in.
Selvage cords: processed wool yarn,
handplied, 2z-S, gray, 3-strand twining
Note: woven on circular frame

35

Round Rug 1981

(illus. p. 91)

Provenance: Gloria F. Ross, 1981;
acquired 1987

1987.85

Dimensions: diameter 36½ in.

Tapestry weave, interlocked joins

Warp: handspun wool, z, natural white,
8/in.
Weft: handspun wool, z, natural white,
natural blended gray, aniline red, aniline
top-dyed black, 24/in.
Selvage cords: handspun wool,
handplied, z, aniline black, 3-strand
twining
Note: woven on circular frame

36

Alice N. Begay

b. 1940

Pinon, Arizona

Clans: *Ma'ii deeshgiizhnii* (coyote pass people); born for *Naakaii dine'é* (Mexican people)

An untiring weaver, Alice Begay always has at least one rug on her looms. In just four and a half months in 1988, she completed at least ten cross-shaped rugs and several rectangular ones. Even though she has a flock of sheep and goats that she and her husband take to the mountains every summer, she buys processed wool yarn so she can make rugs faster. Begay's Ross collection rug, which measures four feet in each direction, took about nine days of steady weaving.

Used by collectors as table covers or novelty wall hangings, cross-shaped rugs are woven only by a few people. Begay learned how to weave this shape from her grandmother in the early 1960s. Her mother makes only rectangular rugs, which Begay still weaves as a change of pace. And now her ten-year-old granddaughter is making her first little rug of simple stripes.

As Begay explains in a mixture of Navajo and English, neither the cross format itself nor the woven cross motifs have any symbolic Christian meaning, although she and her family are Mormons. She occasionally makes a rug in the asymmetrical shape of a Latin cross; one such rug was commissioned by an out-of-state missionary. Through the 1980s her designs were almost invariably based on Ganado Red patterns, but today she often weaves Two Grey Hills colors and designs. For motif and layout ideas, she sometimes looks at the small, framed rug studies on the walls of Hubbell Trading Post; but usually she relies on her own imagination and her family's suggestions.

While most weavers still work only from mental images, Begay is one of a growing number who sometimes sketch designs on paper. One of her daughters, Sylvia Shay, often draws precise designs on graph paper for her. Kept in a fat loose-leaf notebook for easy reference, the colored-pencil drawings range from simple to elaborate geometric images. Begay also weaves into her rugs the *yé'ii* and *yé'ii bicheii* figures that one of her sons draws.

Begay is especially sensitive about others' copying her work, so she shuns photographs and asks that her weaving techniques not be described. The way she sets up her loom to make cross-shaped rugs is a secret she shares with no one outside the family. Although she has won many prizes for these unusual rugs and weaves nearly all the time, she is cautious about appearing proud or arrogant; she feels this might bring trouble to her and her family. Her husband, Willie, who builds her looms and helps adjust the tension, explains, "We've got stories about these rugs, lots of stories. But she doesn't like to tell them. She's superstitious about it. Someday she might teach the younger ones, but right now she just keeps them to herself." Many Navajo women consider their knowledge an important private possession that should not be freely shared lest it be abused or wasted. Begay and her husband liken this to the sandpainter's sacred knowledge, which dedicated apprentices pay to learn.

Cross Rug 1988

Provenance: Hubbell Trading Post, Ganado, Arizona; acquired June 1988

1988.86

Dimensions: 119.5 x 121.0 cm. (46½ x 47 in.)

Tapestry weave, dovetailed and interlocked joins

Warp: handspun wool, z, natural white, 8-9/in.
Weft: processed wool yarn, z, aniline red, natural white, aniline black, aniline blended gray, 15/in.
Selvage cords: processed wool yarn, 3z-S, natural white, 2-strand twining

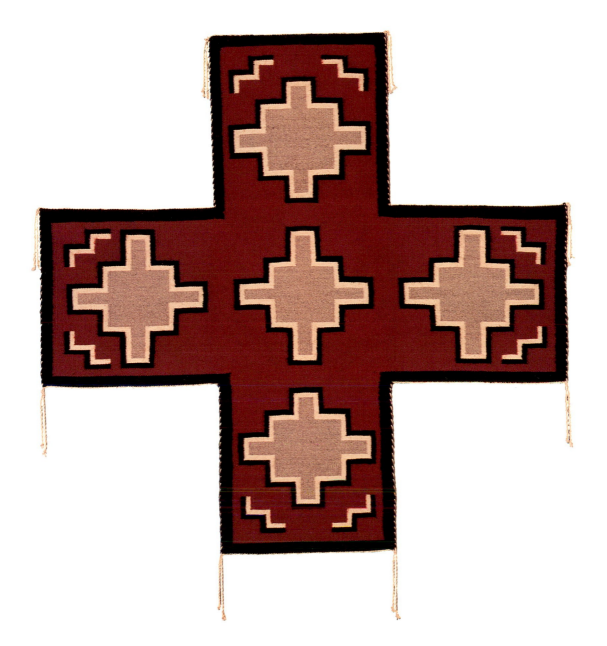

37

Lillie Walker

b. 1929

Coal Mine Mesa/Tuba City, Arizona

Clans: *Kiyaa'áanii* (towering house people), born for *Naakaii dine'é* (Mexican people)

The rugs Lillie Walker made in the 1980s look and feel more like 1930s rugs because of their simple geometric patterns, limited color range, and rough texture. When she wove this rug, Walker was still spinning and dyeing her own yarn, and her colors were soft and muted. Her daughter, Cecilia Nez, who weaves well but doesn't make her own yarn, commented with admiration, "My mother still does the whole thing—shearing, carding, dyeing, and weaving. It takes a lot of planning and concentration." The raised outline technique Walker uses in her Ross collection rug shows her thick, nubby yarn at its best: each diagonal literally stands out.

Walker and her husband still maintain a home near Coal Mine Mesa, east of Tuba City, though they have already sold most of the sheep that once provided wool for Walker's rugs. The settlement for the Navajo-Hopi land dispute gives them only a "life estate" interest in the property. They will be the last of their family to live there, and their children have already relocated. The processed yarn Walker uses now that she no longer keeps sheep has given her rugs a new character.

Despite a fond attachment to her land and home at Coal Mine Mesa, Walker often weaves at her daughter's tiny frame house in a crowded residential area of Tuba City. "My mother doesn't like to weave at Coal Mine Mesa," Nez explains. "There's no one else there weaving. Here, she has company." As Walker and Nez weave side by side on their looms, relatives drop in to chat, children bounce in and out, and puppies and kittens tussle on the floor.

The steady rhythm of weaving provides a pleasant background for the women's conversations. The talk often turns to issues of money, serious business in a family with many children. As more and more Navajos are forced to relocate, jobs are even scarcer in Tuba City than they used to be. Speaking in Navajo mixed with English, the weavers discuss how much someone sold her rug for, what the next rug will bring, whether there's money in getting your picture in a museum catalog, what clothes the children need for school, whether the parts on hand can fix a truck that won't start. The weaving and talking may go on all day. Sometimes a man comes in for food or to see if his wife is in, but this house, dominated by several looms and large boxes of yarn, is clearly the women's domain.

Raised Outline Rug 1988

Provenance: Cameron Trading Post, Cameron, Arizona; acquired May 1988

1988.85

Dimensions: 180.0 x 101.5 cm. (71 x 40 in.)

Tapestry weave, diagonal joins with raised outlines (2-span floats)

Warp: commercial yarn, 4z-S, natural white, 7/in.
Weft: handspun wool, z, natural brown-black, vegetal blue-gray, natural white, vegetal gold, aniline top-dyed black, 22/in.
Selvage cords: warp—handspun wool, 2z-S, aniline top-dyed black, 2-strand twining; weft—paired outer warps

38

Larry Yazzie

b. 1955

Tuba City/Coal Mine Mesa, Arizona

Clans: *Naakaii dine'é* (Mexican people); born for *Kiyaa'áanii* (towering house people)

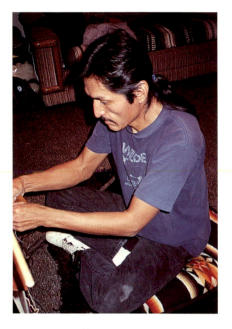

In Larry Yazzie's extended family, both men and women are prolific weavers. More than a dozen of the women weave, and Yazzie's stepfather, brothers, brother-in-law, and several male cousins have all woven excellent rugs. An uncle specializes in unusual saddle blankets. And Larry himself has begun teaching the next generation. He has dedicated his Ross collection rug to the memory of his late brother Andrew, whom Yazzie describes as "an excellent weaver, better than I am."

Even though weaving has generally been considered women's work, Navajo men have made rugs from time to time. More than a century ago, Washington Matthews noted that one of the "best artisans in the tribe" was a man (1884:385). Medicine man Hosteen Klah had to

construct oversized looms for the exceptionally large (twelve by twelve feet) sandpainting patterns he began weaving around 1919 (Newcomb 1964).

At the urging of his mother and grandmother, Larry Yazzie made several small rugs before he started school. "I studied four years of art in school. I used to scribble and draw designs, but not for rugs; I had no idea I was going to be weaving. I finished school and then worked at the high school cafeteria for two years. Then . . . I was in the army for six years. When I got out, there were no jobs in the field I was trained in, so I just stayed at home. My sister said I should try weaving, so she set me up and instructed me. It took me about two weeks to learn all the techniques and ideas. Then I was on my own. Now, it's an okay living for me. That's all I do—I weave full time."

Yazzie has won blue ribbons for his work, which elaborates old-style raised outline designs, borrows figures from Teec Nos Pos and Two Grey Hills regional styles, and packs intricate motifs into tight spaces. Although Yazzie has explored some unusual formats, like the extra-long hall runners he and his sisters make, he especially likes experimenting with color. "After I finished school, I took night classes in art here in Tuba for about three years. That's what I think helped me in my weaving. Mixing the colors of the wool and thinking up designs. Weaving is part of art. Instead of holding the paintbrush, you use yarn and wool."

The unusually large number of male weavers in Yazzie's extended family can be traced directly to the Navajo Relocation Program that followed settlement of the long-standing Navajo-Hopi land dispute. In the mid eighties, most of the Yazzie family was moved from Blue Canyon in the "Joint Use Area" near Coal Mine Mesa. Leaving their livestock behind, they relocated to

newly built houses in Tuba City and the Sanders area. Those, like Yazzie, who went to Tuba City found a serious job shortage. Some turned to weaving to support their families. Those who moved to Sanders found a better job market and an enthusiastic local trader, Bruce Burnham, who encouraged male weavers and successfully promoted the transplanted Coal Mine Mesa raised outline rug as the "Newlands" regional style. Yazzie credits both Burnham and buyer Dan Garland with the ready market his rugs have found since 1985.

Weaving may gain further popularity among men as it becomes more lucrative and reservation jobs remain scarce. An informal reservation-wide survey conducted between 1977 and 1982 identified at least twenty-four men and boys as weavers; there are now undoubtedly many more. People in almost every reservation community know at least one local man who weaves. "Pitching in . . . [so] you can put food on the table and clothes on the family's back— it's like any job," Yazzie says. "My grandmother and mother used to say, 'You should learn to weave, and it will support you.' Budget cuts and job shortages, our grandmother foresaw it all."

Teec Nos Pos
Raised Outline Rug 1991

Provenance: Garland's Navajo Rugs, Sedona, Arizona; acquired August 1991

1991.761

Dimensions: 168.0 x 80.0 cm. (67 x 32 in.)

Tapestry weave, diagonal and vertical with raised outlines (2-span floats)

Warp: processed wool yarn, z, natural white, 10/in.
Weft: processed wool yarn, z, natural and pre-dyed vegetal colors, 34/in.
Selvage cords: warp—processed wool yarn, handplied, 3z-S, gray, 2-strand twining; weft—plain

GLOSSARY

The emphasis on materials and processes in this section underscores the importance of these categories to Navajo weavers themselves. Over and over, weavers stress that insight into their world begins with understanding the significant thought and effort that goes into shearing, carding, spinning, dyeing, and weaving (Hedlund 1989a, 1989b). The definitions apply specifically to contemporary Navajo weaving and may have other meanings in other contexts.

aniline dyes   family of synthetic dyes made originally from coal-tar derivative; first synthesized 1857. Earliest known aniline-dyed yarns in Navajo textiles were raveled from commercial cloth and date to 1860s. Aniline-dyed, machine-spun yarns were readily available in the Southwest by 1870s, powdered aniline dyes by 1880s. (Wheat n.d.)

batten   flat, broad stick usually one or two inches wide and 18 to 36 inches long, used in Navajo and Pueblo weaving to open and maintain the weaving shed between warps while inserting wefts; rarely used by Navajos to beat weft yarns into the weave.

bayeta (also *baize*)   generic term for several types of trade cloth that 19th century Navajo weavers unraveled to use as wefts.

beading   small-scale all-over pattern of dashed lines or blocks made by alternating two different colored wefts in a weft-faced fabric (or warps in a warp-faced fabric). See Marjorie Spencer (14).

bííl (Navajo)   traditional Navajo dress; made of two identical rectangular panels sewn together at both shoulders and sides and worn belted; characterized by solid brown or black center panel, wide red end borders, often with dark blue terraced motifs. Still worn on special occasions.

bilagáana (Navajo)   any Euro-American; from the Spanish, *Americano*.

blanket   rectangular fabric, usually softly woven for draping around the body or use as bedding; replaced by commercial blankets by late 19th century, when Navajo weavers began making rugs.

blend   color made by carding several colors together, most commonly a gray made by combining natural black-brown and white.

Burnham   rug style established 1980s; derived from Two Grey Hills colors and layout, with additional pictorial elements and characteristically compressed appearance; named for community in northeastern part of reservation. See Bessie Barber (12).

Burntwater   rug style featuring vegetal colors, dominant central panel (often a diamond or double diamond), and multiple borders; established 1960s; named for community in south-central part of reservation. See Philomena Yazzie (18) and Jennie Thomas (19).

carders   pair of flat or slightly curved, rectangular brushes with handles and wire teeth set closely in rows; used to clean and align fibers before spinning.

carding   process of cleaning and aligning wool fibers before spinning by brushing with carders.

chief blanket   style of Navajo "wearing" blanket woven wider than long with two zones of wide brown-black and white bands separated by series of narrower blue, black, and/or red bands along ends and across the center; often with diamonds, rectangles, or other geometric motifs in 3 rows of 3 motifs each. The woman's version is distinguished primarily by its smaller size and use of narrow black and gray bands instead of wide brown-black and white bands. See Grace Henderson Nez (1).

Chinle   rug style with banded patterns in vegetal colors; characterized by relatively simple motifs and color combinations; established by 1930s; named for community in central part of reservation.

churro wool   long, lustrous wool with little grease or crimp; easy to work by hand and found most often in pre-1880 blankets. First introduced from Andalusía by Spanish in 1598, churro sheep were gradually replaced by other breeds. A recent breeding program has renewed interest in them.

Coal Mine Mesa   rug style in raised outline weave in many patterns and color combinations; isolated examples from 1930s; established 1950s; named for community in western part of reservation. See Lillie Walker (37) and Larry Yazzie (38).

comb   forklike wooden handtool with 5 or more blunt tines for packing weft yarns into the weave and pointed handle for positioning yarns before packing.

commercial yarn   machine-spun, usually industrially dyed yarn.

Crystal   rug style with banded patterns in vegetal colors; characterized by use of wavy lines; established 1940s; named for community in east-central part of reservation. See Irene Clark (15) and Ella Rose Perry (17). **Early Crystal** rug style contrasts sharply with contemporary Crystal style. It has bold, central pattern and border; usually gray, black, white, and red (fig. 4); established 1897-1911; named for community in east-central part of reservation.

Diné'é (Navajo)   literally, *the People*; the Navajo people or tribe.

dye   any colorant fixed permanently to fibers. **Synthetic dyes**, including anilines, are chemically manufactured; **native dyes** come from natural, nonsythesized animal, vegetable, and mineral sources; **vegetal dyes** make use of plant materials—leaves, flowers, fruits, twigs, bark, roots, etc.

eye dazzler   rug style (1880-1910) with small, serrate triangles and diamonds, often outlined, in intense, contrasting colors (fig. 2). Most use commercial Germantown yarns, but some use handspun yarns colored with synthetic dyes. Precursor of Teec Nos Pos/Red Mesa serrate outline style.

face   textile surface; fabric may be (a) double-faced, with two identical faces; (b) single-faced, with only one "right" side; (c) two-faced, with two faces that do not look alike. Most Navajo rugs and blankets made in tapestry weave are double-faced; that is, the two faces are identical in structure and appearance.

float   portion of weft that passes over two or more warps without interlacing; used, for example, in twill, two-faced, and raised outline weaves.

Ganado (also *Ganado Red*)   rug style with dominant central panel (usually a diamond or double diamond) and at least one border; dark red, gray, black, and white color scheme; established by early 1900s; named for community in south-central part of reservation. See Elsie Jim Wilson (5).

Germantown yarn 3- and 4-ply commercial yarn colored with aniline dyes; originally made in Germantown, Pennsylvania. Three-ply yarns first issued to Navajos in 1864 and replaced by 4-ply yarns in mid 1870s (Wheat n.d.).

handspun yarn usually spun on shaft-and-whorl spindle or on hand- or treadle-operated spinning wheel.

heddle stick and string device on a loom that creates a space between alternate warps so wefts can be inserted and interlaced in one operation.

hogan Navajo house, usually one room and one story, approximately circular in floor plan, with 6 to 8 sides, single door, and domed or pointed roof with central smoke hole or chimney.

join juncture between two colors where a yarn change is made in tapestry weave. **Interlocked join** links wefts of adjacent color areas together by turning around each other between adjacent warps. **Dovetailed join** connects these wefts by turning around a common warp and not each other. **Slit join** leaves a slit between color areas; wefts of two different colors turn around adjacent warps and do not interlock or dovetail together. **Diagonal join** leaves less conspicuous slit by offsetting slit joins progressively along a diagonal.

Klagetoh rug style with dominant central panel (usually a diamond or double diamond) with at least one border; gray, dark red, black, and white color scheme; established alongside Ganado Red style; named for community in south-central part of reservation. See Elsie Jim Wilson (5).

lazy line subtle diagonal line caused by interlacing wefts to join adjacent warp sections woven at different times. Lazy lines allow weavers to avoid reaching all the way across a wide fabric with each pass of the weft. See background of Ason Yellowhair's rug (23). World-wide, few weavers use lazy lines—in the American Southwest, only the Navajo, Zuni, and Mayó Indians.

loom upright rectangular frame that supports the warps.

maquette (also *cartoon*) in European weaving, the model for a woven image; rarely used by Navajo weavers.

Moki stripes (also *Moqui*) design of alternating dark blue and black (or brown) bands, used alone or interspersed with white and/or red bands, sometimes with superimposed diamonds or other geometric motifs (fig. 6). See Gloria Begay (3). The term *Moki* derives from an early, sometimes pejorative, name for

the Hopis although they rarely made blankets with this design (Wheat, personal communication).

natural color color of undyed, untreated wool fibers; generally, shades of white, gray, brown, and black.

plain weave fabric structure in which each weft passes over one warp, then under the next warp in a regular 1/1 (over-one/under-one) sequence; in weft-faced plain weave, wefts conceal warps; in warp-faced plain weave, warps conceal wefts.

ply continuous strand of spun fibers twisted together to make yarn; in combination, indicates number of strands used (*3-ply*).

processed wool commercially cleaned and carded sheep wool formed into continuous strand of loose fibers ready to be drawn and spun (for technical discussion of materials in contemporary Navajo rugs, see Hedlund 1987:83-94).

processed wool yarn single, loosely twisted strand of wool, commercially manufactured but resembling native handspun yarn; sometimes called "prespun" by reservation traders.

raised outline weave variation of tapestry weave in which two colors of weft alternate in pattern areas; wefts skip two warps instead of one at color junctures, thus creating a raised outline around each motif. See Lillie Walker (37) and Larry Yazzie (38).

respun yarn that has been retwisted, usually on a handspindle, to strengthen and smooth it.

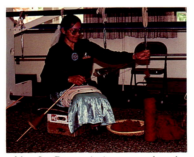

Mary Lee Begay spinning processed wool roving, Visitors Center, Hubbell Trading Post, Ganado

roving continuous strand of slightly twisted fibers (about diameter of pencil) that has been separated from the thicker sliver preparatory to spinning.

saddle blanket small textile used under a saddle to prevent it from galling the horse. Standard single saddle blankets measure 30 in. sq., double saddle blankets 30 x 60 in.; frequently used as small rugs.

sandpainting design elements, motifs, and design layouts traditionally drawn in colored sand, earth, and ground pigments by Navajo medicine men during curing rituals (fig. 9).

sarape (also *serape*) rectangular blanket woven longer in warp direction than in weft direction, about 6 or 7 ft. long and 3 to 4 ft. wide (fig. 1, 5). Draped over shoulders or around the body as outer garment until late 19th century.

sash belt long, relatively narrow fabric woven in a warp float pattern weave and worn as a belt.

selvage (also *selvedge*) edge of fabric where wefts loop around side warps and reenter fabric to weave in reverse direction (side selvage) and where (as in Navajo and Pueblo textiles, which typically have 4 selvages) the warps are uncut and loop around the end wefts ("end selvage").

selvage cords two or more multiple-ply yarns twisted together while interlacing with and reinforcing a fabric's edge. Navajo weavers usually twine two 3-ply selvage cords together to form a 2-strand edge, but the highest quality rugs often have three 2-ply selvage cords.

serrate design sharply pointed zigzag pattern made by diagonals, often used to create diamond shapes.

sliver continuous strand of loose, untwisted fibers obtained by carding, usually several inches in diameter.

spindle long pointed stick and disk-shaped whorl (fly-wheel) used to twist fibers into yarn.

spinning process of drawing out and twisting fibers to form a yarn. The two possible directions of spin are noted by the letters S and Z with the angle of spin in a yarn represented by the slanting direction of each letter's central portion. The following notation is used:

z or s	single-ply z-spun or s-spun yarn;
Z or S	direction of final twist of multiple-ply yarn;
2z-S	z-spun, S-twist, two-ply yarn; comparable notations are 2z-Z, 2s-Z, and 2s-S;
3z-S	z-spun, S-twist, three-ply yarn; comparable notations are 3z-Z, 3s-Z, etc. (Kent 1985:117).

stripe technically, a stripe extends in the direction of warps while a band is oriented horizontally in direction of wefts.

tapestry textile made with very thin yarns in tapestry weave; thread counts of 90 or more per inch. Also refers to textile used as wall hanging. "*Superfine* tapestry" refers specifically to yarn size and quality of spinning and weaving.

tapestry weave weft-faced plain weave with patterns formed by different colored, discontinuous wefts; weavers use several techniques to connect adjacent color areas (see *joins*).

Teec Nos Pos rug style with dominant central panel and multiple borders; characterized by outlining around figures and brilliant color accents; established early 1900s; named for community in northern part of reservation. See Bessie Lee (8).

Teec Nos Pos/Red Mesa Outline multicolored rug style with central panel of overall zigzags and other finely outlined serrate motifs; one or more borders; developed from Germantown eye dazzlers of late 19th century; named for two neighboring communities in northern part of reservation. See Mamie Begay (9).

thread count number of threads in given segment of fabric, usually recorded as warps or wefts per inch (or centimeter); indicates density and relative fineness of fabric.

Three Turkey Ruins rug style with central panel (usually a diamond or double diamond) and border; vegetal colors, especially yellows and greens; established 1970s; named for prehistoric rock art site south of Canyon de Chelly. See Helen Bia (20).

top-dye to apply dye to already colored or dyed material; *e.g.*, when black dye is applied to natural dark brown-black wool.

tops (also *combed sliver*) form of processed wool in which fibers lie roughly parallel to each other in contrast to *carded sliver* in which fibers spiral loosely around the length of the strand.

tufted weave technique in which long fibers or pieces of yarn are inserted into fabric during weaving. See Amy Begay (31).

twill weave float weave in which wefts pass over two or more warps; floats for each successive pass usually aligned diagonally. Most common interlacement among Navajo weavers is 2/2 (over-two/under-two). In **diagonal twill weave** floats progress in one direction with overall diagonal effect. In **diamond twill weave** floats diverge to form series of nested, diamond-shaped patterns (see Irene Julia Nez [33]), and in **herringbone twill weave** they alternate directions to form zigzag pattern.

twining technique in which sets of two or more yarns are twisted together while enclosing a second set within each turn or half-turn. In Pueblo and Navajo weaving, all 4 selvages have a set of selvage cords that are twined about each other while enclosing either the looped warps or wefts.

two-faced weave float weave in which two sets of wefts are interlaced on one set of warps so that the fabric's two faces appear entirely different; interlacement is usually 3/1 and 1/3 (over-three/under-one, under-three/over-one). See Audrey Wilson (29).

Two Grey Hills rug style with dominant central panel (often a diamond or double diamond) and one or more borders; natural gray, brown, black, and white color scheme; established 1920s (fig. 7); named for community in east-central part of reservation. See Daisy Tauglechee (10) and Barbara Ornelas (11).

warp parallel yarns that are strung on a loom. Weft yarns are woven over and under the warps. In completed Navajo rugs, the warps are hidden by the wefts.

wavy lines small-scale pattern of thin horizontal pinstripes that appear to undulate slightly; woven by alternating two different colored wefts in weft-faced fabric (or warps in warp-faced fabric); found especially in Crystal rug style. See Irene Clark (15).

weaver's pathway (also *spirit line*) thin, colored line extending from center design field to outside edge of some rugs; often placed near upper right corner and same color as center field's background. Offers path of escape for energy and spirit put into rug so weaver can weave again (Bennett 1974).

weft yarns that are woven over and under the warp yarns, which are attached to the loom. In completed Navajo rugs, only the wefts are visible.

Wide Ruins/Pine Springs rug style with banded patterns in vegetal colors; characterized by numerous serrate diamond motifs and frequent, but subtle, use of beading; established late 1930s (fig. 8); named for two neighboring communities in southern part of reservation. See Marjorie Spencer (14).

wool fibers from sheep fleece; Navajo term for handspun yarn.

yarn fibers twisted together in a continous length. Navajo use of this term is generally restricted to commercial products; handspun yarn is usually called "wool" to distinguish it from commercially made yarn.

yé'ii (Navajo) special class of supernatural beings with close spiritual relationship to Navajo people and their natural environment; often depicted in stylized anthropomorphic form. *Yé'ii* rugs show front-facing figures, standing singly or in rows. See Audrey Wilson (29).

yé'ii bicheii ceremony 9-day winter ceremony in which *yé'ii* dancers appear; literally, *yé'ii bicheii* means "grandfather of the *yé'ii* (holy people)" and refers to one of the dancers, also called "Talking God," *Yé'ii bicheii* rugs depict semi-realistic figures in profile, usually standing in action poses. See Isabell John (25).

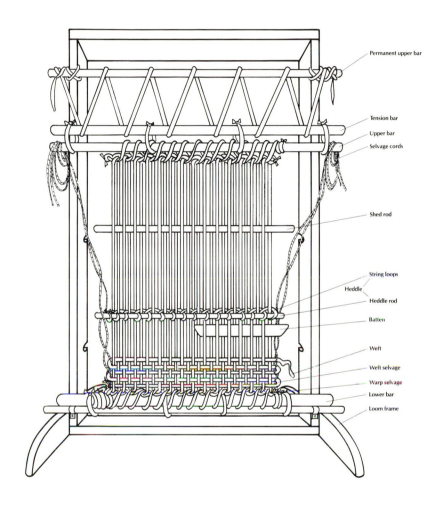

Permanent upper bar

Tension bar

Upper bar

Selvage cords

Shed rod

String loops

Heddle

Heddle rod

Batten

Weft

Weft selvage

Warp selvage

Lower bar

Loom frame

N A V A J O   L O O M

BIBLIOGRAPHY

Aberle, David F.

1961   The Navajo. In *Matrilineal Kinship*, ed. David M. Schneider and Kathleen Gough, 96-201. Berkeley: University of California Press.

1963   Some Sources of Flexibility in Navaho Social Organization. *Southwestern Journal of Anthropology* 19 (1): 1-8.

1982   The Future of Navajo Religion. In *Navajo Religion and Culture*, ed. D. M. Brugge and C. J. Frisbie, 219-231. Santa Fe: Museum of New Mexico.

Ames, Michael

1986   *Museums, the Public, and Anthropology: A Study in the Anthropology of Anthropology*. Vancouver: University of British Columbia Press.

Amsden, Charles Avery

1934   *Navaho Weaving, Its Technic and Its History*. Santa Ana, California: Fine Arts Press. (Reprinted by Rio Grande Press, Chicago, 1964).

Arizona Highways

1974   *Arizona Highways* 50 (7), special issue on Southwest Indian weaving.

1976   The American Way. *Arizona Highways* 52 (7): 14-15, cover.

Bailey, Lynn R.

1980   *If You Take My Sheep: The Evolution and Conflicts of Navajo Pastoralism, 1630-1868*. Pasadena, California: Westernlore Publications.

Bauer, Liz

1987   Research for a Catalog of the Navajo Textiles of Hubbell Trading Post. NEH Grant GM-22317-84. Ms. in author's files.

Bennett, Noel

1973   *Genuine Navajo Rug—Are You Sure?* Santa Fe, New Mexico: Wheelwright Museum of Navaho Ceremonial Art and the Navajo Tribe.

1974   *The Weaver's Pathway: A Clarification of the "Spirit Trail" in Navajo Weaving*. Flagstaff, Arizona: Northland Press.

1979   *Designing with the Wool: Advanced Navajo Weaving Techniques*. Flagstaff, Arizona: Northland Press.

1987   *Halo of the Sun: Stories Told and Retold*. Flagstaff, Arizona: Northland Press.

Bennett, Noel, and Tiana Bighorse

1971   *Working with the Wool: How to Weave a Navajo Rug*. Flagstaff, Arizona: Northland Press.

Bingham, Sam, and Janet Bingham

1976   *Navajo Chapters Government Handbook*. Chinle, Arizona: Rock Point Community School.

1987   *Navajo Chapters*, rev. ed. Tsaile, Arizona: Navajo Community College Press.

Bowen, Dorothy Boyd, and Trish Spillman

1979   Natural and Synthetic Dyes. In *Spanish Textile Tradition of New Mexico and Colorado*, comp. and ed. N. Fisher, 207-211. Santa Fe: Museum of New Mexico Press.

Brody, J. J.

1976   *Between Traditions: Navajo Weaving toward the End of the Nineteenth Century*. Iowa City: University of Iowa Art Museum.

Brugge, David M., and Charlotte J. Frisbie, eds.

1982   *Navajo Religion and Culture: Selected Views*. Santa Fe: Museum of New Mexico.

Bryan, Nonabah G., and Stella Young

1940   *Navajo Native Dyes: Their Preparation and Use*. Washington, DC: U. S. Department of the Interior, Bureau of Indian Affairs, Department of Education.

Clifford, James

1988   *The Predicament of Culture: Twentieth-Century Ethnography, Literature, and Art*. Cambridge: Harvard University Press.

Conn, Richard

l979   *Native American Art in the Denver Art Museum*. Denver, Colorado: Denver Art Museum.

Dedera, Don

1975   *Navajo Rugs: How to Find, Evaluate, Buy and Care for Them*. Flagstaff, Arizona: Northland Press.

Diné Be'iina'

1987-present   *Diné Be'iina': A Journal of Navajo Life* 1 (1)-present. Shiprock, New Mexico: Navajo Community College.

Dockstader, Frederick T.

1987   *The Song of the Loom: New Traditions in Navajo Weaving*. New York: Hudson Hills Press.

Dominguez, Virginia

1986   The Marketing of Heritage. *American Ethnologist* 13 (3): 546-555.

Eaton, Linda B.

1989   A Separate Vision. *Plateau* 60 (1), special issue. Flagstaff Arizona: Museum of Northern Arizona.

1990   *A Separate Vision: Case Studies of Four Contemporary Indian Artists*. Museum of Northern Arizona Bulletin 58.

Eck, Norman K.

1982   *Contemporary Navajo Affairs*. Rough Rock, Arizona: Navajo Curriculum Center, Rough Rock Demonstration Center.

Eckert, Jerry, Edward Knop, Jesse Lopez, and Steve Helmericks

1989   *Employment and Incomes in the Navajo Nation: 1987-88 Estimates and Historical Trends*. Fort Collins: Institute for Distribution and Development Studies, Colorado State University.

Emery, Irene

1966   *The Primary Structures of Fabrics*. Washington, DC: The Textile Museum.

Erickson, Jon T., and H. Thomas Cain

1976   *Navajo Textiles from the Read Mullan Collection*. Phoenix, Arizona: Heard Museum.

Faich, Ron

1981   Summary Results of the 1980 Census in Navajo Tribal Chapters within the Navajo Reservation. Ms., Library of Economic Development, Navajo Tribal Offices, Window Rock, Arizona.

Farella, John R.

1984 *The Main Stalk: A Synthesis of Navajo Philosophy*. Tucson: University of Arizona Press.

Getzwiller, Steve

1984 *Ray Manley's The Fine Art of Navajo Weaving*. Tucson, Arizona: Ray Manley Publications.

Gill, Sam D.

1981 *Sacred Words: A Study of Navajo Religion and Prayer*. Westport, Connecticut: Greenwood Press.

Hedlund, Ann Lane

1983 Contemporary Navajo Weavers: An Ethnography of a Native Craft. Ph.D. diss., Department of Anthropology, University of Colorado, Boulder.

1987 Commercial Materials in Modern Navajo Rugs. *Textile Museum Journal* 1986 25:83-94.

1988 Current Trends in Navajo Weaving. *Terra* 26 (5): 15-20. Los Angeles, California: Los Angeles County Museum of Natural History.

1989a In Pursuit of Style: Kate Kent and Navajo Aesthetics. *Museum Anthropology* 13 (2): 32-40.

1989b Designing among the Navajo: Ethnoaesthetics in Weaving. In *Textiles as Primary Sources: Proceedings of the First Symposium of the Textile Society of America*, ed. John Vollmer, 86-93. Minneapolis, Minnesota: Minneapolis Institute of Arts.

Hedlund, Ann Lane, and Louise I. Stiver

1991 Wedge Weave Textiles of the Navajo. *American Indian Art* 16 (3): 54-65, 82.

Hirschmann, Fred

1989 Crownpoint Auction. *Native Peoples* 2 (2): 2-9.

Iverson, Peter

1983 *The Navajo Nation*. Albuquerque: University of New Mexico Press.

James, H. L.

1988 *Rugs and Posts: The Story of Navajo Weaving and Indian Trading*. West Chester, Pennsylvania: Schiffer Publishing Co.

Jules-Rosette, Benetta

1984 *The Messages of Tourist Art*. New York: Plenum.

1990 Simulations of a Postmodernity: Images of Ethnology in African Tourist and Popular Art. *Society for Visual Anthropology Review* 6 (1): 29-38.

Karp, Ivan, Christine Mullen Kreamer, and Steven D. Lavine

1992 *Museums and Communities: Debating Public Culture*. Washington, DC: Smithsonian Institution.

Karp, Ivan, and Steven D. Lavine, eds.

1991 *Exhibiting Cultures: The Poetics and Politics of Museum Display*. Washington, DC: Smithsonian Institution Press.

Kent, Kate Peck

1985 *Navajo Weaving: Three Centuries of Change*. Santa Fe, New Mexico: School of American Research Press.

Kluckhohn, Clyde, and Dorothea Leighton

1974 *The Navajo*, rev. ed. Cambridge: Harvard University Press.

Lamphere, Louise

1977 *To Run after Them: Cultural and Social Bases of Cooperation in a Navajo Community*. Tucson: University of Arizona Press.

Matthews, Washington

1884 Navajo Weavers. *Bureau of American Ethnology Annual Report, 1881-1882*, 371-391.

Maxwell, Gilbert

1963 *Navajo Rugs—Past, Present & Future*. Palm Desert, California: Desert Southwest.

1984 *Navajo Rugs—Past, Present & Future*, rev. ed. Edited by Bill Bobb and Sande Bobb. Santa Fe, New Mexico: Heritage Art.

McNitt, Frank

1962 *The Indian Traders*. Norman: University of Oklahoma Press.

Mera, Harry Percival

1975 *Navajo Textile Arts*, 2d ed. Edited by Roger and Jean Moss. Santa Barbara, California: Peregrine Smith.

Moore, J. B.

1987 *The Catalogues of Fine Navajo Blankets, Rugs, Ceremonial Baskets, Silverware, Jewelry & Curios, Originally Published between 1903 and 1911*. Albuquerque, New Mexico: Avanyu Publishing.

Myers, Fred

1991 Representing Culture: The Production of Discourse(s) for Aboriginal Acrylic Paintings. *Cultural Anthropology* 6 (1): 26-62.

Navajo Nation, The

1988a *Navajo Nation Fax 88*. Window Rock, Arizona: Commission for Accelerating Navajo Development Opportunities, The Navajo Nation. September 1988.

1988b *A Business Plan for Establishing a Navajo Tourism Initiative*. Window Rock, Arizona: Commission for Accelerating Navajo Development Opportunities, The Navajo Nation. May 1988.

Navajo Tribe, The

1972 *The Navajo Nation Overall Economic Development Program*. Window Rock, Arizona: Office of Program Development, The Navajo Tribe.

1974 *The Navajo Nation Overall Economic Development Program*. Window Rock, Arizona: Office of Program Development, The Navajo Tribe. July 1974.

1979 *The Navajo Nation Overall Economic Development Program*. Window Rock, Arizona: Office of Program Development, The Navajo Tribe.

1980 *The Navajo Nation Overall Economic Development Program, 1980 Annual Progress Report*. Window Rock, Arizona: Division of Economic Development, The Navajo Tribe. October 1980.

1988 *The Navajo Nation Overall Economic Development Program, 1988 Annual Progress Report*. Window Rock, Arizona: Commission for Accelerating Navajo Development Opportunities, The Navajo Tribe. September 1988.

Newcomb, Franc Johnson

1964 *Hosteen Klah: Navaho Medicine Man and Sand Painter*. Norman: University of Oklahoma Press.

Pendleton, Mary

1974 *Navajo and Hopi Weaving Techniques*. New York: Collier Books.

Pepper, George H.

1923 Navaho Weaving. Ms. in files of the National Museum of the American Indian, New York.

Plateau

1981 Tension and Harmony: The Navajo Rug. *Plateau* 52 (4), special issue. Flagstaff, Arizona: Museum of Northern Arizona.

Reichard, Gladys

1934 *Spider Woman*. New York: Macmillan. (Reprinted as *Weaving a Navajo Blanket* by Dover, New York, 1974).

1936 *Navajo Shepherd and Weaver*. New York: J. J. Augustin. (Reprinted by Rio Grande Press, Glorieta, New Mexico, 1968).

1939 *Dezba, Woman of the Desert*. New York: J. J. Augustin.

1950 *Navaho Religion: A Study of Symbolism*. New York: Pantheon Books. (Reprinted by Princeton University Press, Princeton, New Jersey, 1970).

Rodee, Marian

1981 *Old Navajo Rugs: Their Development from 1900 to 1940*. Albuquerque: University of New Mexico Press.

1987 *Weaving of the Southwest*. West Chester, Pennsylvania: Schiffer Publishing Co.

Roessel, Ruth, comp.

1970 *Papers on Navajo Culture and Life*. Tsaile, Arizona: Navajo Community College Press.

Roessel, Ruth

1981 *Women in Navajo Society*. Rough Rock, Arizona: Navajo Resource Center, Rough Rock Demonstration School.

1983 Navajo Arts and Crafts. In *Handbook of North American Indians*. Vol. 10, *Southwest*, 592-604. Washington, DC: Smithsonian Institution.

Saltzman, Max, and Nora Fisher

1979 The Dye Analysis and Introductory Remarks. In *Spanish Textile Tradition of New Mexico and Colorado*, comp. and ed. N. Fisher, 212-216. Santa Fe: Museum of New Mexico Press.

Shepardson, Mary, and Blodwen Hammond

1970 *The Navajo Mountain Community: Social Organization and Kinship Terminology*. Berkeley: University of California Press.

Stocking, George W., Jr., ed.

1985 *Objects and Others: Essays in Museums and Material Culture*. Vol. 3, *History of Anthropology*. Madison: University of Wisconsin.

Sunset Magazine

1987 The Land of the Navajo and Hopi. *Sunset Magazine* 178 (5): 97-109.

Tsá'ászi'

Tsá'ászi' Magazine. Quarterly student publication of the Pine Hill School, Pine Hill, New Mexico.

Vergo, Peter

1989 *The New Museology*. London: Reaktion Press.

Waldman, Diane

1977 *Kenneth Noland: A Retrospective*. New York: Solomon R. Guggenheim Museum, with Harry N. Abrams, Inc.

Walters, Harry

1977 *Navajo Weaving: From Spider Woman to Synthetic Rugs*. Tsaile, Arizona: Navajo Community College.

Wheat, Joe Ben

1976 Navajo Textiles. In *Fred Harvey Fine Arts Collection*, 9-47. Phoenix, Arizona: The Heard Museum.

1977 *Patterns and Sources of Navajo Weaving*. Denver, Colorado: Harmsen's Western Americana Collection.

1978 *Navajo Blankets, Australian Exhibition 1978-79*. Netley, South Australia: Art Gallery of South Australia and the Australian Gallery Directors' Council Ltd.

1981 Early Navajo Weaving. *Plateau* 52 (4): 2-8.

1984 *The Gift of Spiderwoman: Southwestern Textiles, The Navajo Tradition*. Philadelphia: The University Museum, University of Pennsylvania.

n.d. Blanket Weavers of the Southwest: Pueblo, Spanish and Navajo. Ms. in progress, files of the author.

Wilkins, David E.

1987 *Diné Bibeehaz'áanii: A Handbook of Navajo Government*. Tsaile, Arizona: Navajo Community College Press.

Witherspoon, Gary

1983 Navajo Social Organization. In *Handbook of North American Indians*, Vol. 10, *Southwest*, 524-535. Washington, DC: Smithsonian Institution.

Wyman, Leland

1970 *Sandpaintings of the Navaho Shootingway and the Walcott Collection*. Smithsonian Contributions to Anthropology, no. 13. Washington, DC: U.S. Government Printing Office.

Young, Robert W., comp.

1961 *The Navajo Yearbook: 1951-1961, A Decade of Progress, Report no. 8*. Window Rock, Arizona: Navajo Agency, Bureau of Indian Affairs, U.S. Department of the Interior.

Young, Robert W., and William Morgan

1981 *The Navajo Language: A Grammar and Colloquial Dictionary*. Albuquerque: University of New Mexico Press.